BEATLES, BEATMAKERS, MERSEYBEAT, AND ME

KARL TERRY

BEATLES,
BEATMAKERS,
MERSEYBEAT,
AND ME

PHARAOH PRESS

Beatles, Beatmakers, Merseybeat, and Me

ISBN 978-1-901442-50-2

First Published in 2020 by Pharaoh Press
www.liverpoolbooksonline.co.uk

Design and typesetting by Ian Hughes, www.mousematdesign.com
Edited by Peter Etherington, www.takeawaycopy.com

Printed and bound by CPI Group (UK) Ltd, Croydon, CR0 4YY

Wednesday, 18th January, 1961

A winter night in Liverpool. It was freezing cold and blowing a gale but I couldn't feel a thing. None of us could. We were so pumped full of adrenaline we could hardly think straight. You see, for a bunch of likely lads in a rock 'n' roll band, this gig was the stuff dreams were made of. The possibilities were endless! As we travelled to the venue in our battered Bedford Workobus, we dreamt up fanciful scenarios for the night ahead. But none of us could've predicted what would actually happen.

The second we came to a stop in Mathew Street, we were mobbed by screaming girls. We could barely open the van doors. Wow! I wound down the window and asked what they were after. Autographs? Photographs? Phone numbers? "No," they replied, "Cliff Richard!" Needless to say, Cliff Richard was not in our van, but the young crowd had every reason to think he might be. The Shadows, Cliff's world-famous backing band, were playing a one-off gig at The Cavern Club, and hopes were high that Cliff would sneak in for an impromptu appearance.

The Shadows weren't the only band taking to the stage that night. Middle of the bill were The Remo Four, who were fast becoming a breakout success in Liverpool. There was a real buzz around them, and rightly so. But before these great bands went on, there would be a young group who were auditioning at The

Cavern Club for the first time ever. That was me and my band; an assembly of rock-crazed teenagers known as Karl Terry and The Cruisers. Wow! Wow! Wow!

In early 1961, The Shadows were probably the biggest band that had ever visited Liverpool; certainly the biggest to play The Cavern. When we found out that our audition fell on the same night that they and The Remo Four were playing, we were blown away. Every single band in Liverpool would be eating their hearts out. They'd kill for this. But it was *our* night and we were determined to make the most of it. Particularly with The Shadows' management looking on.

Once the disappointed crowd had dispersed, we started unloading our equipment from the van. Mathew Street, a fruit market by day, was its usual dark, dank self. The sweet and sour stench of rotten fruit always lingered, and your only escape was the steep, narrow staircase of The Cavern. There was no rear entrance. No matter how famous your band were, every drum, guitar, and amplifier had to be carried down that tight, uneven stairway; made all the tighter by the queue of young music fans waiting to pay their entrance fee at the bottom.

When you reached the belly of the club, rotten fruit gave way to hot, damp, sweat-dripping funk. Then another smell hit you: San Izal. That was the pungent disinfectant they used to mop up the flood from the toilets; a flood that frequently spread to the pockmarked concrete dance floor. That death-trap dance floor was in such bad condition that it that inspired an understated dance step called 'The Cavern Stomp'. It was the only dance step you could safely manage. If you tried anything wilder you were bound to hit a piss-filled pothole and go flying!

The club was already busy when we arrived. Treading carefully, we weaved our heavy gear through the heaving mass of bodies and made our way to the band room. Once there, we discovered that the door, in typical Cavern fashion, opened outwards, making it incredibly awkward to negotiate. A bonus feature was the blind step in front of that door, handily placed for the uninitiated to fall down. And we did. But we'd made it. We were in The Cavern, adrenaline pumping, about to set up our gear with trembling hands.

This opportunity was gifted to us by a legendary figure in Mersey music history: Cavern Club compère Bob Wooler. Bob had previously been a compère at the Aintree Institute, where he'd developed an encyclopaedic knowledge of Liverpool's up-and-coming rock 'n' roll bands. His instinct was that rock was about to eclipse jazz in popularity and he wanted to help in any way he could. So, when he took over at The Cavern, which was more of a jazz venue at that point, Bob began to wrangle auditions for the beat groups that had impressed him. His instinct was right. Conveniently positioned in Liverpool's city centre, The Cavern Club quickly became the beating heart of this new music scene. *Our* music scene. God bless you, Bob!

We waited nervously off-stage, knowing that any second now we'd duck through the damp archway and step out into the spotlights to make our Cavern debut. The place was packed, but the crowd weren't there to see us. They were there for The Shadows and their smart Fender guitars and high-tech amps. That band were the professional pinnacle as far as we were concerned. They'd even been in earlier in the day for a soundcheck. Wowza! What on earth would their audience make of a bunch of mid-teens with a homemade bass amp and a regular guitar tuned an octave lower to masquerade as a bass guitar? We were about to find out.

Bob Wooler approached. "You ready, lads?" We put on our matching jackets and pumped ourselves up. Those jackets, mustard yellow with black lapels and 'Rockin Cruisers' stitched into the back, were our coat of armour. We'd worn them the night we won a big competition at the Liverpool Locarno in 1959. That win put us on the road to our debut at The Cavern, so it was fitting that the jackets came with us. They always made a good impression. In fact, one of those jackets is on display in The Museum of Liverpool to this day!

Bob gave us a big introduction and, to mild applause, we stepped out into the light; yellow jackets beaming. From the first chord, we put everything we had into that thirty-minute slot. I doubt I've performed harder, louder, or with more determination since. I leapt from the stage and took my performance into the audience; dancing wildly among the beatnik-filled seats at the front. To say the crowd went wild would be pushing it, but I didn't care. I was going to make 'em have it! Them and everyone else.

After a procession of Gene Vincent numbers that fit us like a glove, we were breathless, sweat-drenched, and ready to drop. As our last note echoed around the damp brickwork, Bob took over the mic and asked the crowd to give it up. A ripple of polite applause and muffled conversation greeted us from the seats at the front. But at the back of the long archway, in the gloom beyond the glow of the spotlights, we heard wild cheers and screams. People had space to dance back there and they'd clearly got into it. After all, this wasn't music to sit and study, this was music to dance to! Perhaps we hadn't brought the house down as we'd planned, but we got the feeling we'd won some fans. More importantly, those fans came to watch The Shadows, but now Karl Terry and The Cruisers was the name on their lips. What a high!

Our performance was over, but our night wasn't. Far from it! With space at a premium, we had to haul our gear back to the van. If you thought it was hard to go down The Cavern's stairs with a bass drum, try going up 'em! We were shattered by the time all of our kit was safely back in the Workobus, but we weren't going to miss The Shadows! We returned to the club to watch the main attraction and hang out with the band members; half hoping to get a tap on the shoulder from The Shadows' management.

While The Remo Four were busy thrilling the crowd that night, we played an unwitting part in one of The Cavern's immortal moments. My band and I were wide-eyed, music-mad teens, so it was only natural that we'd want to hang out and chat with Hank Marvin and the rest of The Shadows. Doing my best to play it cool, I'd struck up a conversation with Hank in the band room. But that chat was brought to an abrupt halt by a big commotion outside. Before we could investigate, the commotion came to us.

Jet Harris, The Shadows' handsome bassist, was blind drunk. How he made it down The Cavern's stairs I'll never know, but, as he staggered towards the band room, swearing and slurring, he fell down the blind step and hit his head on the outward-swinging door. My bandmates and I helped him inside then quickly made ourselves scarce. This was mortifying for everyone involved. Even with our limited experience, we knew what it felt like to have someone in the band let you down. Performance demands focus, and anything that throws you off your stride is bound to show on stage. Particularly if your bassist, the anchor of the band, is three sheets to the wind!

Asking around, we learned that Jet had filled his boots across the street at The Grapes. There was no alcohol served in The Cavern Club in those days, so The Grapes pub was a famous haunt for thirsty musicians. I've certainly spent many happy hours in there over the years. Clearly, Jet's happy hour had gone on a bit too long! The Shadows kept their professional cool and agreed to play, regardless. So, with an expectant crowd hanging on his every word, Bob Wooler introduced this giant of a band. Hank Marvin, Tony Meehan, and Bruce Welch stepped out to a rapturous reception and got ready to play. Meanwhile, a group of us helped Jet Harris onto the stage and propped him up against the piano. We couldn't watch!

The Shadows put on a brave face that night, but it was a miserable experience. In addition to a drunken, misfiring bassist, their sound balance was completely off because their soundcheck took place when the venue was empty, giving a false acoustic. It was clear that the cramped confines of The Cavern were a world away from the dance halls and theatres they were used to. This also meant that, perhaps most disappointingly, there wasn't room for the band's famous walking dance steps. Not that they didn't try. In fact, while we were hiding away in the band room, we heard yet another commotion outside. Apparently, during an attempt at a walking dance step, Jet Harris carried on walking and fell off the stage.

Travelling home in the van that evening, it was hard to take it all in. The excitement of playing The Cavern for the first time, even to a mixed reception, had given us such a high. But witnessing first-hand what the music business had done to Jet Harris and The Shadows, we couldn't help but wonder... Would that be us? We were teenagers having a blast right now, but how long would it last? The Shadows were only a few years older than us.

Those thoughts were quickly brushed aside as the gigs came thick and fast following our Cavern debut. Three weeks later, on Thursday 9th February, The Beatles played their first gig at The Cavern; a lunchtime session. They got a mixed reception too, but it didn't matter. The buzz was building and we could sense that this was the start of *our time*. Of course, in hindsight, it was The Beatles' time. In those early days however, our bands were equals in an electrifying new music scene; a scene the whole world would come to know as 'Merseybeat'. But how did I end up slap bang in the middle of it?

Early days in Liverpool

The world of rock 'n' roll knows me as Karl Terry, but to my family and old school friends I'll always be John Connor. Terrance John Connor, to be exact. My aunt had a fondness for the name John, so that's what everyone called me. And I mean *everyone*. I didn't find out my real first name was Terrance until I took my eleven plus exams! It's probably just as well I didn't go around calling myself Terrance. Where I grew up, having a posh name like that would definitely make your life a little bit harder. I had it hard enough already.

I was born in 1942, the middle of the Second World War, and grew up in Kensington, Liverpool; an area that felt the full effects of the war and the deprivation that followed. Of course, like all Scousers, my family made the best of a bad situation and the war just became another factor in our daily lives. It's certainly a feature of my earliest memories. I recall, as a child of about two years of age, amusing my family by sitting inside a dining chair and opening and closing the removable seat like I was operating a tank turret. I called this contraption my 'Bongerina'! That memory comes from our time on Moorgate Street near Wavertree Road in Edge Hill, and I realise now that it's my first memory of being the centre of attention.

We soon left the Edge Hill area and moved a mile north to

Patteson Street in Kensington. While I have little recollection of my early years in Kensington, I do remember playing outside of the air-raid shelter in Patteson Street. Incidentally, this road was among several that were bulldozed and replaced by a new development in the 90s. Would you believe the roads of this new development are all named after The Beatles? These guys, who I performed with and hung out with, now have streets, airports, and even asteroids named after them! It boggles the mind.

* * *

People aren't lying when they say that times were tough in our part of Liverpool. But for us kids, everything was an adventure. Whether we were crawling through the bushes in Newsham Park or racing our steering carts down 'Donkeys Hill' on Lister Drive, we used our imagination to bring our adventures to life. One minute I'd be a cowboy hero like Johnny 'Mack' Brown, Hopalong Cassidy, or The Durango Kid, and the next minute I'd be Robin Hood or Dan Dare. I've always been attracted to flashy names.

When I was a bit older, my friends and I would go to the local cinemas. There were plenty to choose from in those days. Among our favourites were the Palladium, Cosy, Litin (nicknamed 'The Flea Pit'), Savoy, Casino, Kensington, and the Majestic. No matter where you went, a trip to a Saturday matinee was a big event. Our street gang would buy penny-bags of broken cakes, along with some 'sticky lice' and a bit of sherbet. And, we'd get a cinnamon stick to smoke if we were hard up for cigarettes. To scrape together the money for these outings, I used to haul fish boxes home from Great Homer Street Market or The Old Haymarket, chop them up, tie them in bundles, and sell them as firelighters. Alternatively, I'd collect empty jam jars and beer bottles and take them back to the shops for a refund. The *other* way into a cinema was to pool our money and gain admission for one person. Then, as soon as the lights went down, our man on the inside would push the safety bar on the exit door and let the whole gang in for free. We called this 'bunking in'.

The end of the war brought new sights and sounds to the city. Liverpool echoed with sound of street singers performing like they were at the Milan Opera House, newspaper sellers shouting "Excee Echo!", and the warming brass tones of the Salvation Army Band. I have fond memories of 'rag-and-bone' men exchanging old clothing and scrap metal for goldfish and ex-army guns. We played 'Cowboys and Indians' with *real* rifles that we could barely lift!

For a treat, my family would take me to the Pavilion Theatre on Lodge Lane. There I saw the acts that inspired my early interest in music. Among the best were Hetty King, Wee Georgie Wood, and the bubbly Tessie O'Shea.

* * *

As a boy growing up in our working-class area, you had your life mapped out for you. Leave school, learn a trade, work hard, raise a family, and expect your sons to do the same. Pursuing a different path wasn't common. So, when I took an interest in music in my teens, my family assumed it was just another phase and pushed me to get an apprenticeship. I'm glad they did, it's served me well. For my friends and I, however, music was different to, say, football or cricket. None of us *really* believed we could be sports stars; the chances were just too slim. But when we saw musicians like Lonnie Donegan blazing a trail, it opened a new world of glamorous possibilities. The thing is, unlike sports, music wasn't a big part of our education, so we'd have to learn the hard way.

My school journey started at Saint Michael's Infants on York Street, West Derby Road. I finished twenty-third out of twenty-four pupils in my class but somehow managed to win a scholarship to Saint Francis Xavier's. This was followed by a stint at Evered Avenue Technical College. Being in the Catholic minority meant I had to work even harder to fit in. I chose to gain acceptance through something we all had in common, football. It was hard work, though. Our sports teacher had incredibly high standards; he was the England schoolboys' coach at the time! When I asked him how to improve my left foot control, he replied: "wear a bed slipper on your right foot and you'll soon learn." Boy, did I learn fast! Those old leather balls were so hard and heavy, particularly when wet, that I nearly broke my foot with the first kick! Not to be beaten, I went on to represent the school at junior, intermediate, and senior level as an 'outside left'.

Life as a sporting attention seeker had its drawbacks. I entered myself in the school's inter-house swimming gala just so I could take part in the neat dive competition. Why the neat dive competition? Classes at Evered Avenue were mixed, which meant girls! As those girls would almost certainly be watching the gala from the gallery, it was the perfect chance to impress. What I noticed about the diving contest was that contestants lost points if they looked down as they approached the towel at the edge of the pool. So, when it was my turn, I strode out like a peacock; always looking up and taking my time to hook my toes over the pool edge. Full of confidence, I burst into a glorious swan dive and entered the water like an arrow. Impressive stuff! Only, at this point, my teammates had to dive in and rescue me as I hadn't learned to swim yet.

This incident was the start of a lifelong friendship. One of my rescuers that day was John Dickson. Not long after dragging me out of the swimming pool, John helped me to form my first skiffle band; playing a washboard, tea-chest bass, and even a one bar electric fire along the way. He later became my manager too. So *this*, as they say in all the good stories, is how it all began. Except, in my case, it ain't no story, it's the truth!

Teddy boys and skiffle bands

Every Sunday morning between the hours of ten and twelve noon, youngsters aged eleven to sixteen would congregate in their 'Sunday best'. During these meet-ups, I noticed that a new style was filtering into the older boys' dress code. They were abandoning the traditional blazers, neckties, and grey flannel trousers in favour of drape jackets with jetted half-moon or patch flap pockets. To this, they were adding velvet collars and cuffs, very tight 'drainpipe' trousers, thick crepe-soled shoes, and 'slim-jim' neckties. The 'Teddy Boys' had arrived! In case you ever wondered, they were called Teddy Boys because their dress code was influenced by the dandies of the Edwardian period; 'Teddy' being a nickname for Edward.

This fashion statement mirrored the musical revolution that was taking place. Our parents admired Johnny Ray, Ruby Murray, and Perry Como, but that was old hat as far as we were concerned. For us, this was 'Bill Haley and The Comets' time! Then, just as we were getting used to tracks like 'Green Tree Boogie' and 'Ten Little Indians', Lonnie Donegan kicked the door open with 'Rock Island Line'. Now we, the kids, had found our sound. This was the early nineteen-fifties; considered the 'trad-jazz' and beatnik period. With that in mind, who would've thought that the man who'd truly change the face of British pop music would be playing the banjo?! Lonnie Donegan and His Skiffle Group were a huge hit. And when Lonnie swapped to guitar, British teenagers gained an idol who is still worshiped by me and millions of other musos to this day.

Thanks to Lonnie, kids up and down the country were painting tea chests and borrowing their mum's washboard and sewing thimbles! And, of course, *everybody* wanted a guitar. They didn't want one as badly as me, though. So, while my friends were getting new pushbikes, I got a Hofner guitar. No one in my street gang believed I had it, so I promised them a demonstration. Later that day, a fleet of kids on new bicycles gathered in our concrete garden (which we called an 'airy') to peer into the front room of the house while I performed. Of course, I didn't know anything about 'concert pitch' or 'frets' at this point, I just wanted to be Lonnie!

Our wind-up gramophone cabinet in the living room was so rarely used that my mum put a large Aspidistra plant on top of it! I removed the plant, wound up the gramophone and placed a dusty seventy-eight RPM on the deck. Then, nearly strangling myself with the piece of string I had for a guitar strap, I opened the curtains and hip swivelled away to... Anne Shelton's 'Lay Down Your Arms'. Boy, did I look a fool? Wow! The kids laughed, but at least they all knew that I had a guitar.

* * *

Showmanship aside, fitting in was still a challenge. We were the only Catholic family in my street and I had no father. To make things worse, I was a college pudding who had to walk through the neighbourhood every day wearing a school cap and a blazer jacket while carrying a satchel full of books. I was never going to be the new Lonnie Donegan looking like that! But this didn't stop me from diving into this exciting new musical world. By the age of thirteen, I was hanging around with older boys in the emerging coffee bar scene. The jukebox was loaded with skiffle tunes and the latest American releases, so our soundtrack was Paul Anka's 'Diana', The Vipers' 'It Takes A Worried Man' and 'Maggie Mae', not to mention tunes from artistes like Frankie Vaughan, Russ Hamilton, Slim Whitman, Jerry Colona, and even Nervous Norvus with his novelty song, 'Ape Call'.

One night, a rumour spread that there was going to be a gang fight at the funfair in Newsham Park, so we all went along. I don't recall if there actually was a fight, but at that fair I heard a song by the great Carl Perkins that I later found out was called 'Honey Don't'. It blew me away! And didn't all the American singers and movie stars have fabulous names? The more of this new music I heard, the more I liked it. This was definitely for me.

My world began to revolve around the music of Marvin Rainwater, Sonny James, Jerry Lee Lewis, Buddy Holly, Little Richard, and Fats Domino. That music has stayed with me my whole life. I even recorded Fats Domino's hit, 'I'm Gonna Be A Wheel Someday', on an album called *Mersey Survivors* in the late 70s. Of course, I was a big fan of Elvis at the time too, but my true hero was Gene Vincent. Gene is, and always will be, my favourite singer. The man's voice was so versatile; exploring an unbelievable vocal range at a time when most singers were just trying to be Elvis. Then again, who wouldn't want to be Elvis? What a voice! And what a repertoire! Only recently, The Cruisers and I recorded 'That's All Right Mama' and 'Baby Let's Play House', which I've been singing for nearly fifty years. If only I could get near The King's voice!

As the music spread, it was only natural that we Brits started to develop our own rockers. Tony Crombie, Tommy Steele, Terry

Dene, and Don Lang were all pale imitators of the great American stars, but they paved the way for the likes of Vince Taylor, Marty Wilde, and our big breakthrough, Cliff Richard. Cliff led the way with tracks like 'Move It', 'High-Class Baby', and 'Dynamite'. These great rock 'n' roll tunes have never received the recognition they deserve. They gave hope to myself and hundreds of other aspiring musicians; inspiring us to learn and copy what they were doing in order to make the same breakthrough.

4

The first stage

My first experience of performing happened almost by accident. After the war, we had wild house-parties in Liverpool. These parties became known as 'jars out', which was a similar concept to what the Americans called 'barrelhouse'. In preparation for these house-parties, we'd go to the local pub with empty bottles, jugs, or flagons and return with enough beer for the night's party. The most important item on both sides of the Atlantic, after the beer, was the piano. No piano, no party. And, as everyone was expected to sing a song, even a kid like me, I stepped forward and sang an Al Jolson number. Warbling my tonsils at this audience and being the centre of attention gave me such a rush. Wow! My first introduction to performing got me hooked for life. I belonged on stage.

There's a saying: musicians find musicians. But if I was going to become one, I needed to learn how to play my instrument. Especially as I'd already convinced my friends, John Dickson and Reggie Lewis, to play the washboard and tea chest in my skiffle band. I reached out to my distant cousin, Jackie Bishop, too. He was studying classical guitar at the Pierre Bethel studios in Islington. Our band, we decided, would be called The Gamblers. We glued some playing cards onto our painted tea chest and set out to topple the kings of skiffle! We even had our own signature tune, 'Gamblin' Man'. Of course, this was one of Lonnie Donegan's biggest hits, but we planned to write and record our own songs one day. As it happens, it would be another forty-five years before I could record any of my own songs.

With Jackie on hand to tune my guitar and teach me the basics, I soon learned all of the major skiffle songs. Now I was ready to give Carl Perkins a run for his money! At least I thought I was. Born under the Pisces star sign, I've always been a bit of a dreamer. But time was moving on and so was the music. Having failed to win approval at several talent contests and auditions in working men's clubs, I got the chance to travel to Eastbourne to holiday with John's relations. This would prove to be the next phase of my musical education.

Being two likely lads from Liverpool, we asked the bus driver if we could sit in the front seats. We played our guitars all the way to Eastbourne; treating the other passengers to strangled versions of 'Railroad Bill', 'Maggie Mae', 'Love Is Strange', 'No Other Baby But You', and 'Sixteen Tons'. Then, after what seemed like an eternity, we arrived! Once we'd had a good night's rest, we went to see what Eastbourne's coffee bars had to offer. This was the day I truly discovered Elvis Presley. He was on the jukebox churning out guitar solos, slap double bass, and *drums*. Wow! And isn't 'Tutti Frutti' just the most stunning rock 'n' roll tune?! But how did he get that sound? I was determined to find out. Another lesson from our trip to Eastbourne was that washboards were out and drums were in! Also, I desperately needed an amplifier.

Finding an amplifier wasn't a problem, but the size of the one I found was. My Broadway amp was a little cream and red box with an on/off switch, a volume knob, and a tone knob. Maximum output: eight measly watts. Everybody was going Elvis crazy, but I couldn't even get near the voice, never mind the guitar sound. I had to find a style and sound that suited me; something similar to Elvis, but more obscure.

Six months previously, our teacher had asked our class if anyone would like to correspond with an American magazine called Oregon Journal Juniors, which I did. Out of curiosity, I asked my pen-pal about American rock 'n' roll. She sent me a photo of Gene Vincent! I'd never heard of him, but he looked so cool! I was determined to get my hands on one of his records. Though, this was more challenging than you'd imagine. Despite the skiffle and rock 'n' roll boom, most record stores still catered for traditional, grown-up record buyers searching for the big dance bands and ballad singers of the post-war era. They weren't catering for the emerging buying power of 'the teenager'.

So, when yours truly swaggered into Phillips, the long-established music store on Kensington off of Low Hill, asking about the latest Gene Vincent releases, I must've been a huge nuisance to Mr Phillips. I can only imagine what he made of me; a scrawny teenager decked out in drainpipe trousers that looked more like jodhpurs because I'd taken them in at the bottom but hadn't sewn them in tight above the knee. That's in addition to my Tony Curtis hairstyle; complete with what we called a D.A. (duck's arse) parting at the back. Perhaps he thought a Martian had landed?

This shop, Phillips, would go on to become the famous 'Percy Philips Studio and Record Store' where The Beatles recorded their first demo. As I've mentioned, nobody realised there was going to be a huge teenage record market. Like my family, everybody assumed it was just a passing phase. But my pestering, along with other like-minded kids, helped people like Mr Phillips to see the potential in Liverpool's emerging music scene. Still, in those early days, if you wanted anything other than a run-of-the-mill record you had to order it from the store. I did just that and, two agonising weeks later, I was the proud owner of Gene Vincent's 'Blue Jean Bop'. I still have the same copy!

This was it! A style and sound that was me to a T. That record was played and played until I'd memorised every word, phrase, drum beat, guitar riff, and bass pattern. But no matter how many times I played it, I couldn't recreate Gene's sound; not even close. The problem had to be the amplifier. I persuaded a friend of a relation to inspect my little Broadway amp. This guy had been in the Royal Air Force working on their radar system. Wow! He arrived at my house a couple of nights later and duly listened while I cranked up the old record player and played 'Blue Jean Bop' a couple of times. He quickly got a feel for the sound I was trying to imitate. His professional opinion? If I wanted to sound like 'Galloping' Cliff Gallup, Gene Vincent's lead guitarist, all I needed to do was put a layer of greaseproof paper between the loudspeaker and the speaker cloth. No way?!

Being an aspiring rock 'n' roll star cum pseudo-Teddy-Boy, I'd assumed I needed a flashy new guitar (maybe a Gretsch or Fender Telecaster) and a new amp (maybe a big Gibson or a Fender Twin Reverb). But no. I needed to raid my mum's baking supplies! Boys being boys, out came a screwdriver and a hammer and, a few beers later, my little cream and red Broadway sounded like... a kazoo! Now *that's* progress! I should mention that, by this point, I'd swapped my Hofner guitar for a turquoise Rosetti 'Lucky 7'. The Rosetti had single cutaway that made it look like Bert Weedon's guitar. I assumed this would make it easier to play. In reality, the finger-board action was so high I would've needed a hand like The Incredible Hulk to get past the third fret! But did it look flash?! Wowee! That guitar came everywhere with me.

Performing alongside P.J. Proby at
The Navy Club in Liverpool.

Me and Bobby Jones, who was a
member of my first skiffle group.
Check out my big quiff and
matching 'duck's ass' hairstyle!

A photo from my trip to
Eastbourne with John Dickson
(left) in the late 50s.

Fifteen years-old and so proud of
my flash guitar!

Lance Railton, me, Arthur Rigby, Alan Swanson, and Tommy McGuire at Newsham Park.

A farewell party for the American singer-songwriter P.J. Proby, hosted by The Beatles' first manager, Alan Williams. Pictured beside me (left) are Rufus from the Blue Angel Club, P.J. Proby, Mavis Railton, and my old mate Lance Railton.

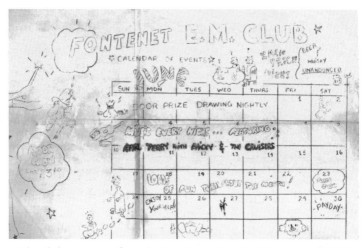

A hand-drawn poster from the American airbase in Chateauroux, 1961.

Our line-up at the airbase featured me (right centre), Geoff
Caddick on bass, Gordon Templeton on drums, and our
chanteuse Nicolette 'Nicky' Moran.

A gig at the Aintree Institute in Liverpool; featuring Wally Shephard on base, Ritchie Galvin on Drums, Dave Gore playing rhythm, Lance Railton on lead guitar, and me in my flashy tartan jacket providing the vocals.

What a line-up! This is a flyer for a special gig at Liverpool Stadium on May 3rd, 1960. This stadium was a large indoor venue; not to be confused with Liverpool's football stadium, Anfield.

JACARANDA ENTERPRISES
. . . . BY ARRANGEMENT WITH LARRY PARNES

THE GREATEST SHOW EVER TO BE STAGED
IN ENGLAND

LIVERPOOL STADIUM

Tuesday, May 3rd at 8 p.m.
(THREE HOUR PROGRAMME)   DOORS OPEN 7-30 P.M.

GENE VINCENT

Davy Jones

ITALY'S NERO AND HIS GLADIATORS
with the fabulous NEW SOUND from Italy

Lance Fortune   PYE HIT PARADE, "BE MINE"

Peter Wynne   Julian X

The Viscounts

Colin Green   Billy Raymond
AND THE BEAT BOYS   YOUR HOST & COMPERE

PLUS Liverpool's CASS AND THE CASSANOVAS
RORY STORM AND THE HURRICANES
JERRY AND THE PACEMAKERS
MAL PERRY AND RICKY LEA
JOHNNY & THE JETS   DERRY & THE SENIORS

PRICES: — 10/- — 7/6d. — 5/- — 3/6d.
Tickets available from Lewis's, Cranes, Rushworth's, Beaver Radio, Frank Hessy., The Stadium, Top Hat Record Bar, Dale St., the Jacaranda Coffee Bar, and Nem's.

A bunch of likely lads at the Star Palast in Darmstadt, Germany. Beside me (left) are drummer Paul Hitchmough, bassist Gordon Loughlin, saxophonist Mike Evans, and guitarist Lance Railton.

The poster for our gig at the Northwich Memorial Hall in 1963, supporting The Beatles no less!

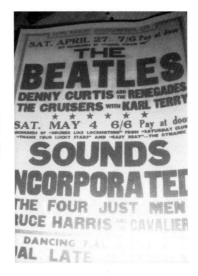

Here's me and Les Braid, of The Swinging Blue Jeans, at the Blue Angel Club. Les was a member of one of my first bands, Terry and The Teen Aces.

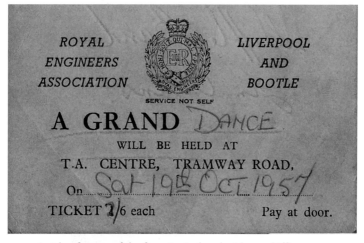

A ticket for one of the first gigs I played with my skiffle group, The Gamblers.

An article about Cilla Black, featuring a snap of me sitting next to Cilla's good mate, Christopher Biggins!

Bill Haley and His Comets played the Odeon Theatre in Liverpool on February 20th, 1957. Here's my ticket stub and accompanying autographs from the band! Their performance that night convinced me to follow a career in music.

Gerry Clayton, me, Gordon Templeton, and Dave Hamilton playing at the Barnton British Legion in 1963.

My official pass for the Airmans Club in La Martiniere, France, in May 1962.

Me and my fresh-faced bandmates in 1960.

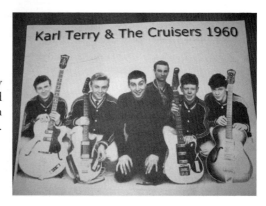

5

The dawn of Merseybeat and The Beatles

Bands were forming all over Liverpool, but mine desperately needed a drummer. Without one, our group members were becoming frustrated. So frustrated that one guy left to join a Norwegian navy expedition as a cabin boy. You could do this once you reached sixteen years of age and it would land you a trip to New York. You'd return to Liverpool a few weeks later with a packet of Lucky Strikes, a brash floral shirt, and a Chuck Berry album. I can't say I didn't consider it, but I was having too much fun making music and I knew that, despite being an adventurous spirit, I needed stability in my life. That stability came in the form of a bricklaying apprenticeship. This was a wise decision. Having a trade to fall back on has served me well over the years; putting food on the table during some tough times in the music business.

Despite the upheaval, a recurring theme during this early period was musicians finding each other. For example, the guy who played the tea chest bass in our band knew somebody who played drums. He only had *one*, a tom-tom with a single skin and the snare string on the outside, but it didn't matter. Our band had found it's 'Be-Bop' Harrell! That's a reference to Dickie 'Be-Bop' Harrel, Gene Vincent's drummer, who remains to this day greatest drummer I've ever seen or heard with the brushes.

Now, most people in the music game, from compères to

bandleaders, will tell you that drummers can be quite eccentric. This guy did nothing to change that stereotype, but I'll be forever in his debt as he put me in touch with the great multi-instrumentalist Les Braid, who would become a lifelong friend of mine. Les was a great guitarist and a wonderful boogie-woogie piano player. If anything, he was too good! That's why a professional band quickly snapped him up from under our noses. After very briefly being our 'Galloping' Cliff Gallup, Les went on to deserved fame with the band that poached him, The Swinging Blue Jeans.

When we lost Les, it felt like it might be game over for us. But as luck would have it, living in the same street as our one-tom-tom Gene Krupa was a fourteen-year-old kid who idolised, and could imitate, Cliff Gallup. Wowser! Look out world, this band's cookin'! Or so we thought. We found out the hard way that our eccentric drummer suffered from, among other things, fainting spells. At one memorable gig on the sloping stage at Blair Hall, after an almighty unrehearsed drum-roll, his drum rolled past me into the audience.

It was around this time that my gran started a scrapbook of my band's adventures. This included newspaper clippings, pictures, ticket stubs, flyers, you name it! The rest of the family assumed my musical exploits were just another phase, like stamp collecting, comic books, or playing football. But I think my gran had a sense that this would be something I'd want to look back on, no matter what happened. How right she was, God bless her.

* * *

Some gigs in Liverpool had six or maybe ten different groups on the same bill; all trying to find their style and sound. This explosion of music encouraged more music stores to open. In turn, these stores became meeting places for the growing number of band members. We all wanted to play anything that resembled our American idols but were still working out how to do it. So, to help each other out, we shared new guitar intros, bass lines, and drum breaks we'd been working on. Plus, with the onset of 'top twenty' sheet music, we were able to copy words and chords (often without actually purchasing any goods). It was such a creative and exciting time.

As the competition increased, more venues opened to accommodate our emerging scene and things really began to blow up. Through persistence, our band won a chance to play at one such venue, The Cherokee Club, which was really just a couple of rooms above Johnson's The Cleaners in Bold Street. And they only sold coffee! To win this opportunity, we'd entered a band competition at the Liverpool Locarno in 1959. This competition involved various heats, followed by a semi-final, and then a final which we won! We beat bands like the Four Jays (who later changed their name to The Fourmost) and Faron & The Tempest Tornadoes, whose lead singer would later form Faron's Flamingos. We had no gigs to play, so after every heat we had a full week to rehearse. By the time the final came around, we'd had our flashy yellow stage jackets made and were really well prepared. Still, we never expected to win. This was the start of something big!

Winning the final wasn't the only life-changing event that happened to me that night. I met my future wife, too! When we didn't have a gig, I'd often take her to a club to watch other bands. During one such romantic outing, I was lucky enough to witness the emerging talent of the greatest rock 'n' roll band the world has ever seen. These five charismatic young guys played all the numbers I loved, many of which were B-sides, but they played them in a way that I'd never imagined. Instead of having one singer, this band had four or five! When one sang lead vocals, the rest of the band harmonised or performed unison back up. This was ground-breaking. One of them played a guitar with only four strings, upside-down, and could sing like Little Richard or Peggy Lee. Their rhythm guitarist was as loud as the lead guitarist and could sing like Chuck Berry. The lead guitarist sounded and played like Carl Lee Perkins. The bass player sat down or turned his back to the audience. And the powerhouse drummer wore a stunning purple shirt and was the living image of movie star Jeff Chandler, yet had the moody charisma of James Dean. These guys were different.

Both girls *and* boys went crazy for every single number. This was unusual. In the late fifties and early sixties, most bands consisted of a drummer, a bass guitarist, a rhythm guitarist, a lead guitarist, and a vocalist. But the focus was always on the vocalist, who'd be doing his best Elvis or Cliff Richard impersonation to impress the girls. The problem was, if the singer impressed the girls too much, their boyfriends wouldn't like the group and would probably want to kick the shit out of him given half a chance (as I can well recall). But the distinct personalities of this new group meant that, if you didn't like the drummer for example, there was always someone else in the band to admire. Nobody knew where these lads came from, but the people I spoke to in the audience said the group had posh accents and dressed in a scruffy 'art-school' manner. This venue, by the way, was The Liverpool Jazz Society, which would soon be renamed The Iron Door and go on to rival the iconic Cavern Club.

I didn't hear anything about this group for several months. Then, one night at Litherland Town Hall, a sound came from behind the closed stage curtains that still sends a shiver down my spine. Surely it could only be Little Richard?! Then the compère, Bob Wooler, announced: "Direct from Germany, the fabulous Silver Beatles!" This was the same group I'd seen some months ago, only now they were a four-piece powerhouse combo who wore leather jackets and trousers and sported cool, unruly haircuts. And, boy, were they shit hot! But, *The Silver Beatles*? What an unusual name! We played at a lot of the same venues in the weeks that followed, so I slowly got to know the people behind this snowballing musical juggernaut. The funny thing is, because they were often introduced as "direct from Germany", everyone assumed they were German!

Developing the sound

Writers of Beatles and Merseybeat history have differing opinions on how Merseybeat, as we know it today, originated. For me, it began with hundreds of Scouse skiffle groups all trying to imitate the American sound with improvised equipment. This experience prepared them for the challenges they faced when they inevitably morphed into rock 'n' roll bands; namely sub-standard gear and P.A. systems that were better suited to calling Bingo. Fighting these limitations moulded the Merseybeat attitude and sound, but it also gave us camaraderie. And, as we helped each other by trading tips and techniques, our familiar sound spread across the city like wildfire.

Being big in Liverpool wasn't enough on its own, though. The groups that *really* made a mark honed their craft by playing long, arduous sessions in clubs on the continent. A prime example is The Beatles' legendary period playing the clubs of Hamburg. Those formative months cemented their sound and took their stagecraft to a new level. However, a lot of Merseybeat historians fail to inform their readers that, prior to The Beatles' arriving in Hamburg, there were several other Liverpudlian groups already playing and recording there.

Of those groups, Howie Casey and The Seniors are perhaps the best known. These guys were the bands' band; admired and respected by all of the up-and-coming beat combos in Liverpool and the wider Mersey area. Their lead vocalist was the fabulous Derry Wilkie, who was backed up by a brilliant young man who could sing like Elvis, Ray Charles, Larry Williams, or even Little Richard. That man's name was Freddie Starr. Wowser! On guitar they had Brian 'Griff' Griffiths, who would later achieve fame with a band called The Big Three (a favourite of The Beatles themselves). And, in Frank Wiberly, they had a drummer who, to my mind, was every bit as good as Little Richard's drummer. Of course, leading this unique outfit was the tremendous tenor sax of Howie Casey. These talented guys were unquestionably the forerunners to Liverpool's musical invasion of Germany.

There were other Merseybeat legends established in Hamburg during this period of musical folklore. Kingsize Taylor and The Dominoes were one. The other contained a controversial future Beatle, Ringo Starr! That band was Rory Storm and The Hurricanes, who were without doubt Liverpool's most flamboyant and visual band at the time. I know this first hand as I played fifty-fifty lead guitar with them for a short time. But the Hamburg-based act that I feel had the biggest impact on The Beatles' sound was Tony Sheridan. Tony had close links with The Beatles throughout their time in Germany. The 'fab four' even made a memorable cameo on his hit record 'My Bonnie', which gave record sales a huge boost. It's worth remembering that Tony was a resident at Hamburg's Star-Club long before *any* Merseyside bands arrived. And it's no coincidence that a lot of the bands who played in Germany while Tony was there returned to Liverpool playing and singing very much like him. Tony Sheridan deserves so much more credit for his influence on the Merseybeat sound. Our groups learned so much from him. God bless you, Tony! (And He did).

* * *

The Beatles may have been drawing attention to the Merseybeat scene, but it did little to inspire venues to improve their P.A. systems and general facilities. Even the much-hyped Cavern Club had barely changed since I'd been to watch a performance by Nat Gonella (Britain's answer to Louis Armstrong) when I very first started my original skiffle group! They only had two twelve-inch speakers facing the two exterior aisles of this world-renowned venue, and there were no stage monitors, so every vocalist was essentially flying blind. Funnier still, if a band had more than one vocalist, they had to vie for the best side of the single Reslo microphone. These ribbon microphones always had one side louder than the other, so we had to spin the microphone to find the loudest side. Bob Wooler taught us that trick.

British audio manufacturers weren't paying attention to this new market. So, once again, Scouse bands had no choice but to improvise and build their own kit. Adrian Barber of The Big Three built a guitar and bass cabinet, known as 'The Coffin', that became the envy of all the Merseybeat bands, including The Beatles. This cabinet enabled the trio to deliver a wall of sound! Of course, being a trio without a rhythm guitarist and no echo-unit left a hole in their sound, but they overcame this with the dynamic drumming and vocals of Johnny 'Hutch' Hutchinson and the fabulous improvised bass playing and vocals of Johnny 'Gus' Gustafson. Naturally, as the guitars went up in volume, drummers responded with wooden bass-drum beaters and rivets in their crash and ride cymbals.

For my band, reproducing the sound of our idols with substandard, home-made equipment wasn't our only challenge. With no expertise to call upon, we also had to learn how to style ourselves, promote ourselves, and make our group stand out from the competition. It was trial and error, but I imagine our experiments were similar to those of most Merseybeat bands.

My first major realisation was that the frontmen of the best bands had distinctive names. John Connor wasn't flashy enough, so I looked for a stage name that would set me apart. Inspired by my *real* first name, Terrance, I started to go by Terry Connor. Not that this was much of an improvement! I also changed my band's name from The Gamblers to Terry and The Teen Aces; hoping we'd be the Scouse answer to Frankie Lymon and The Teenagers. This new name didn't last very long, though, as it seemed a bit too sweet. I went back to the drawing board on my name, too.

In the late fifties, inspired by the mystique surrounding the early incarnation of The Beatles, our band members had given each other German nicknames. My nickname was Karl, spelled the German way. I liked the punchy combination of Karl and Terry, so I started going by Karl Terry. Clearly, it stuck! But what about my band? We desperately wanted the flash and glamour of an American group. Of course, in my eyes, there was no one more glamorous than Gene Vincent. His early LP, *Cruisin' with Gene Vincent and The Blue Caps* had a title track called 'Cruisin'', and I'd always loved how cool that sounded. So, with a little encouragement, The Teenagers became The Cruisers and a Merseybeat band was born.

Every frontman has a style, but it takes time to develop. My inspiration came from Rory Storm and performers like him who danced around while their guitarists were playing solos. I worked on my own brand of high kicks and wild dance moves, and would dive into the splits (which I can still do) as a big finale! Anything goes as long as I make it back to the microphone in time! I found that dancing around like this added energy to the band and helped to create my on-stage persona. I became so well known for my stage antics that The Cavern Club compère, Bob Wooler, dubbed me the 'Sheik of Shake'; which I still get called to this day!

Of course, it wouldn't be much of a band without a bass guitar. But with no hope of getting one any time soon, we improvised. After all, isn't a bass guitar just a four-stringed guitar? Problem solved! Take two strings off the rhythm guitarist's Hofner Senator, tune it an octave lower, and wapaloonie! Thing is, this new contraption shook every screw loose in our bassists' seventeen-watt, three-sided, Watkins 'Dominator' amp. Our solution was to go to an ex-army radio spares shop and get all the gear necessary to convert a school desk (inkwell still intact) into a bass speaker cabinet. Lookin' good!

Another problem we faced early on was that no one could hear me, the singer. With no money for a professional microphone, we came up with a solution that involved a Grundig tape recorder microphone, a broom-pole, a roll of Sellotape, a beer crate, and two house-bricks. Suddenly I sounded like Caruso! We improved our stage outfits along the way too. In the beginning, our signature look was black shirts worn with white ties, combined with black trousers (of assorted shades) and scuffed white running pumps. I can only imagine what the bus drivers of the Liverpool and Birkenhead Corporations made of us as we bundled on to their buses with our army kit-bags and polythene-wrapped instruments. Still, like the song says, "things can only get better". And they did. After a couple of years of hard slog, the chance to take our band overseas arrived and we were ready for the challenge!

Cruisin' in France

In 1960, a guy named Harry Lewis arrived in Liverpool looking for bands to entertain the American troops stationed in France. His pitch? "You'll live like a Hollywood movie star, dine on T-bone steaks, and smoke king-size Lucky Strikes!" The clincher? A guaranteed contract of twenty-five pounds a week: paid in dollars! No contest. "Vive la belle France and all the way U.S.A.!" Keen to help us make the most of the opportunity, my uncle, Harry Owens, bought a Bedford Workobus and drove us all to Dover. Did I say "all"? I'll come back to that.

The contract that I'd signed, which insisted that our band would be known as The Wolfgang Combo while playing in France, was made through a Dutch agent who lived in a place called Chateauroux. Looking back, I don't suppose that contract (which I still possess) was worth a dime, but we never gave it a second thought. Destined for Chateauroux, we said goodbye to uncle Harry and his van at the port of Dover. Harry was due at work the next day, despite having driven all night on a six-hundred-mile round-trip with no motorways. God bless you, Harry Owens! While Harry hurtled back to Liverpool, we set sail for France and began our adventure.

* * *

Have you ever tried negotiating with a French railway porter? Try putting a full drum-kit in the passageway of his railroad carriage! Then add three guitars, three amps, and various other bags and suitcases. Negotiations were fairly one-sided, but, somehow, we made it to *gay Paris* with our gear intact. We had to sleep on the floor of the Gare Du Nord station while we waited for our connecting train, but we didn't care. Every inch we progressed got us that little bit closer to "Hollywood".

We arrived in Chateauroux; dishevelled but still full of the American dream. I managed to contact the floor-show boss at the Airmen's Club via a bartender. Pretty soon, the 'Sheik of Shake' and his band were being chauffer driven to the base in a Chevrolet Impala Ranch-Waggon! This kid from Kensington in Liverpool could really get used to this kind of treatment. Wowee! We came back down to earth when the club manager read us the house rules. 'No smoking on stage'?! How was I going to look as cool as Frank Sinatra? As the list of rules went on, it became clear that this was a professional job with a dash of military procedure thrown in for good measure.

From that point on, the problems came thick and fast. The biggest shock came when 'Ace', the guy who ran the whole club, told us to set up for a sound check. What the hell was a sound check? One that didn't bounce? (A bit of Scouse humour for you there). See, in 1960, we Liverpudlian peasants of the realm were still using two-amp three-pin mains plugs. In fact, our family only had two mains sockets in the whole house! One in the downstairs living room and one in the parlour. Everything from electric fires to steam irons and even the radio ran off those two sockets. That radio, by the way, was acquired from the Accumulator Shop and was frequently tuned, with great difficulty, to Radio Luxemburg to listen to the Top Twenty or Dick Barton. Wowser!

Scousers are born improvisers, so we dove right into the sound check. How hard could it be anyway? Well, our English amplification system had an earth wire on the 3-core mains cable, and our amps were set at a voltage of 240. The American system, however, was a 110-volt system and had a ground switch on a two-wire cord. Still with me? Needless to say, when we plugged in and played a little 'Johnny B. Goode', the second I got near the microphone... KABOOM! I can still feel those blisters on my lips today.

Undeterred, our club boss made a phone call and, with some good ol' American know-how, they re-wired the stage and provided a power generator for us. Although, at this point I think Ace might've been wishing he could re-wire the band. We were clearly a man short, voiding our contract. This shortage came about because our guitarist (the one who could imitate Cliff Gallup) couldn't get a passport. Apparently, the officials were reluctant to let an unaccompanied fourteen-year-old work as a musician in France! As ever, if a guitar or bass player can't make a gig, yours truly has to deputise. Which I did. But we were still a man down. To confuse things further, we were assigned a blonde-bombshell singer called Nicolette 'Nicky' Moran. She was there to inspire the troops and add a little spice to our ensemble.

Ace was willing to overlook our manpower shortage as long as The Wolfgang Combo lived up to its entertainment billing with Nicky in tow. In case you're wondering, that name, The Wolfgang Combo, was forced on us because of the contract made with the American Forces Entertainment Office. It was drawn up on the proviso that a band called The Wolfgang Combo would play. This fictitious name was a place-holder to secure the contract, but it was still binding. So, because it wasn't confusing enough already, we presented ourselves as: 'The Wolfgang Combo featuring Karl Terry and The Cruisers with Nicky'!

* * *

Even the lowest ranking soldier was earning a lot more than we were. They also had three square meals a day and were well looked after. Regardless, there were a lot of lonely young men on that base and they were thrilled when they learned that our band all spoke English. They were even more thrilled when they found out that our singer did too. "Well, how y'all doing?" they'd say. "Can I get you guys a drink?" "How do you like American cigarettes?" "You know, you guys sure do speak with a funny accent?"

We realised immediately that the attention we were getting from these lonely young soldiers was just an avenue to chatting-up our singer. With a little bit of military planning of our own, we arranged to sit on separate tables. In doing so, we stood a better chance of some lovesick lothario saying: "Why don't you call your band and the little ol' singer over and have a drink on me?" Of course, we always obliged. Within days, our blonde bombshell became the Vera Lynn of the assembled troops. She fell in love too, which could only mean trouble ahead.

Man, these guys were pleased to be able to converse with us. And I can't tell you how many times we were asked where we learned to speak English! Of course, after explaining that we *were* English, the questions came thick and fast. "Is it true y'all sip tea and eat crumpets?" These conversations led to a barrel of laughs and helped us make some good friends. Among those friends was a young G.I. called Junior, who loved to fool around on the drums. Junior came in handy when our 'agent' sent a photographer to take some promotional snaps of us. We had to think on our feet, otherwise our agent would find out we were a man short! When the photographer came around, I got Junior to sit at the kit with a baseball cap on, head down low, while our own drummer (who fancied himself as a futuristic Django Reinhardt) played our spare guitar. Clever, huh? I even laughed myself. This decision had unintended consequences, though.

Having seen the resulting photos, our agent called to say that if our versatile English drummer was now playing the guitar, he would send a replacement drummer to complete the band. We declined; 'better the devil you know' and all that. As a compromise, he sent a new guitarist who turned out to be a long-lost friend of mine, Pat 'Paddy' Chambers. Paddy and I went *way* back. He was a real musical talent too, and deservedly went on to achieve great things with the legendary trio known as Paddy, Klaus & Gibson. Paddy lent his talent and style to many other great bands, including Faron's Flamingos and John Lennon's 'Plastic Ono Band'. I'm proud to have known such a wonderful boy, man, singer, and guitarist. A true friend.

With the arrival of Paddy, the band was complete again. But we needed to find an apartment for this virtuoso. The Master of Arms at the base knew of a little old lady in a nearby village who would rent a room to singles only and took us to view this *place de résidence*. The old lady took to Paddy like a duck to water and immediately rented her immaculate room to him. As soon as the terms were agreed it was time to party! Long before our first sips of *vin rouge*, I knew this was going to be a special night. Not only had I renewed a good friendship, I'd also gained a talented and innovative band member! Within minutes, Paddy and I were talking about new songs. Our reinvigorated drummer, Gordon 'Frantic Franz' Templeton, was chipping in with ideas too. Three or four bottles of wine and a round of Cognacs later, we threw our empty glasses into the fireplace and were promptly escorted to the exit.

Our night didn't end there. On our way home we stumbled across a fun fair that had dodgems. To three drunken musicians this was too good to resist! At the fair, they had a system of payment that still baffles me today. The method was to purchase a 'duro' at the cash desk and somehow insert it in the dodgem car. We arranged that Frantic Franz would ride in one car while Paddy and I would be in the other. We were having such a ball that, when our dodgems inevitably stopped, Paddy decided to jump out to buy more duros. Only, as he jumped out, he ran straight into another car and went flying! Paddy picked himself up immediately, so we assumed he was okay, but on returning to the dodgem he did remark that he felt like he'd pissed down his leg.

How the hell we managed to get back to Paddy's newly rented room I'll never know, but I can still see him at the front door with a finger across his lips telling us to be quiet. From this point on things become hazy, but I remember wanting to vomit...

As you might imagine, the scene the next morning wasn't pretty. We were woken by the sound of the little old lady screaming: "Allez! Allez! Allez!" She'd walked in on three bleary-eyed musos crammed in a single bed, covered in my vomit, Frantic's shit, and Paddy's blood which had been pouring from his heel after his run-in with the dodgem. We tried to apologise as we rushed around gathering our clothes – picking bits of broken table lamps and vases off as we went. Out in the hallway, we found the light switch sticking out of the wall like a broken umbrella! Not a proud moment.

Paddy received seven stitches in his heel before he'd played a single note for 'Karl Terry and the Boozers', but things seemed to be on the up for our swinging combo. Then, just as the band had finally found its way into the floor-show boss's good books, our singing sweetheart, Nicky, found out that her all-American lover was married! What's a girl to do, slash her wrists? Yep, that's exactly what she did. Twice! As the medical staff on the base weren't allowed to treat employees of the American Armed forces, we had to race to get Nicky to an off-base hospital. These antics got us fired, but our sympathetic agent soon got us another gig. This time we were off to an Army base in Chinon, the town in the Loire valley where Joan Of Arc began her campaign to rid France of *les Anglais*. Perhaps we should've taken the hint.

With blood now safely pumping through the veins of our *chanteuse*, the band played on. Well, "safely pumping" is a stretch. Nicky soon needed to have her appendix removed, which left us a band-member short once again. The show had to go on, so we picked up a few gigs as a four-piece group. But our line-up took yet another hit when our bass player, Geoff, decided to return to Blighty to get married. Thing is, when they found out he was back, the Liverpool constabulary took the opportunity to question Geoff about his bass guitar. Apparently, he hadn't asked its owner if he could: a) borrow it, and b) take it to France! Entertainment is all about characters but this was becoming a 'Carry-On' farce.

Our crafty Dutch agent quickly replaced Geoff with Leo. Leo was a Dutchman who played double bass. He also played the clarinet... through his nose! This guy was no 'Jumpin' Jack Neal, the bass player with Gene Vincent and The Blue Caps, but he was an accomplished musician who could read and write music and soon had me doing the same. Within days we were rehearsing, then performing, one of Sidney Bechet's instrumental hits, 'Petite Fleur'. *Voila!* Leo used to slay the audience with his nose-blowing clarinet numbers, and I used to slay Leo by standing on his upright fiddle in genuine rockabilly style. Wowser!

Our 'agent' made plans for the tour to continue when Nicky was discharged from hospital, but by that point she was the only one who wanted to go on. So, with a fond *adieu*, Frantic Franz and I bummed a ride to *gay Paris* and returned to Liverpool.

8

The Beginnings of Beatlemania

"The Beatles would be bigger than The Shadows within six months and as big as Elvis inside a year." These were the prophetic words of Brian Epstein. His prophecy was first voiced to Gerry Marsden and me, along with various members of other groups, at our daily gathering in The Grapes pub on Mathew Street after a lunchtime session had finished across the road at The Cavern Club. Also hearing it for the first time was Cavern Club compère Bob Wooler, who offered one-pound bets to anyone who disputed Epstein's boast. I'll let you imagine what went into Bob's drink when he went to the toilet.

We had no idea just how big The Beatles would become because we all felt equal back then. In fact, when Merseyside's 'Top Twenty' combos were listed in 'Mersey Beat' magazine in October 1961, Karl Terry and The Cruisers were ranked number seven! The same magazine conducted a more formal ranking in January 1962; decided by a vote among the magazine's readers. That vote is controversial to this day as, when the votes were counted, Rory Storm & The Hurricanes emerged as the number one band. However, after reviewing the postal votes, the organisers noticed that lots of the votes for Rory were from the same part of Liverpool, had same handwriting, and were written in the same green ink. Perhaps it was Rory himself? We'll never know. But those dubious votes were declared void and The Beatles took the top spot. The thing is, it was later strongly rumoured that The Beatles had done exactly the same thing as Rory. They'd just been a bit smarter about it!

In case you're wondering, we were ranked fifteenth in the 1962 poll. I have to pinch myself when I remember that, at one point in time, my band were considered to be almost as fab as the 'fab four'. But The Beatles' stock rose and it rose fast, leaving the rest of the Merseybeat groups clinging to their shirt tails. Even though there was a certain amount of resentment, without their breakout success our fledgling scene may have faded into obscurity. Instead, The Beatles became the beating heart of the music industry and brought our music to the world's attention.

Of course, few people in the music industry knew The Beatles better than the Merseybeat bands. The Cruisers and I played a lot of gigs alongside them and, to us, they came across as well-spoken middle-class lads who'd gone to art school and become studenty beatnik types. They certainly weren't the working-class heroes they're portrayed to be. They had central heating where they grew up!

Did their better upbringing give them a leg-up? Maybe, but they weren't the only middle-class band in Liverpool. What the young Beatles had that others didn't was contacts. They also had a rounded and culture-led education. This came across most in Paul and John who, in addition to being very culturally aware, were witty and had a cynical sense of humour. This often made it hard to keep up with them in conversation and I sometimes came away with the feeling that they were putting me down in a way I couldn't understand. That said, if they did look down their noses at us working-class lads it wasn't obvious. They were fun to be around too.

Pete Best came from the wealthiest family of the original Beatles, but he was different; more approachable and introverted. To me, he came across as a quiet, handsome, thoughtful gentleman who always had time for you. I really felt for him when I learned his band had forced him out. It seemed so sudden and out of the blue. His replacement, Ringo Starr, grew up in a small house in the Dingle area of Liverpool, just south of Toxteth. Even though he was working-class in comparison to his bandmates, they never appeared to hold that against him and really embraced him as a band member. We always got on well with Ringo. He's a nice guy and, whatever you think of his role in The Beatles, he worked really hard to make something of himself after an illness-plagued childhood.

Changing drummers did little to dent The Beatles' popularity. And, as their popularity bloomed into a national sensation, Merseybeat bands scrambled to grab a share of the spotlight by imitating their style. They changed their clothes, their hair, the numbers they were playing and the instruments they were playing them with. Mouth-organs, Hofner bass guitars, and Rickenbacker guitars all got dusted off. As did lots of Gibson 'Jumbo' guitars, which hadn't been seen since the heyday of the Everly Brothers. Our world hadn't been shaken like this since Lonnie Donegan's 'Rock Island Line' debuted.

The imitation game spread beyond Liverpool and bands all over the world began to replicate their style. I remember hearing that Peter Noone, of Herman's Hermits, was mobbed by adoring female fans at his first appearance at The Cavern. A couple of nights later I was lucky enough to be on the same bill as the Hermits in Manchester. That night, I saw that their image had completely changed. This formerly clean-cut band were now wearing leather jackets and had Beatle-style haircuts! This was just the start. It wasn't that long ago that British bands had been copying the look and sound of Elvis and Cliff Richard. Soon, Elvis and Cliff were donning leather to keep up with The Beatles!

9

A crossroads

It strikes me that Pete MacLaine was probably in the right place at the wrong time with his excellent backing band The Dakotas. For reasons I've never fully understood, The Beatles' manager, Brian Epstein, poached The Dakotas to back Billy J. Kramer. He offered Pete a spot with Billy's old backing band in return, but Pete turned him down; even after John Lennon and Paul McCartney had tried to persuade him by offering to write songs for his new band. What Pete didn't know was that Brian had already approached *me* to leave my rockin' Cruisers and front The Dakotas! This happened after a gig at The Queens Hall in Widnes. Brian had booked us to appear alongside The Beatles, Gerry and The Pacemakers, and Pete MacLaine and The Dakotas.

We clearly made an impression at this gig, but it wasn't plain sailing. Our Frantic Franz, through no fault of his own, had a big red boil on his chin. Being an image-conscious group, we convinced him to cover it up with a white dressing and Elastoplast. This seemed like a sound plan. However, the boil plaster came loose when Frantic began to sweat while drumming. He desperately tried to stick it back on and keep his beat. But, in the melee, he somehow caught the handkerchief he used to dampen his snare drum with a drumstick and sent it flying into the air. The handkerchief landed on Frantic's head just as his boil plaster fell off and landed on the snare drum! Poor Frantic. The band powered on, regardless.

Brian Epstein was obviously not deterred. When I went to pick up our fee, which was paid out by Cilla Black in 'Eppy's' office, he asked me if I'd be interested in further bookings? When I replied, "certainly, mister Epstein", he said: "but without The Cruisers." Apparently, he had an excellent professional band to back me. I was thrown, but I immediately rejected his offer; pleading that The Cruisers and I were all friends from the same area and I couldn't desert them. That was on Wednesday or Thursday. On Saturday morning, at The Kardomah Café on Whitechapel, Billy Kramer rushed in to ask why I turned Eppy down. I said that I was an indentured apprentice bricklayer (true) and wanted to finish my apprenticeship (untrue, as proven by my European gallivanting). He said he was also an apprentice on the railways but had taken the offer anyway. It was a tough decision for Billy, because he and his band, The Coasters, were also close friends. Of course, Billy went on to great success with The Dakotas, while The Coasters replaced him with Chick Graham and continued to be managed by Ted Knibbs.

People sometimes ask me if I wonder what my life would've been like if I'd accepted Eppy's offer and joined The Dakotas. It's quite a crossroads in my life after all. Frankly, if I had accepted that offer, I'm pretty sure I'd be dead by now. After honing their act in Hamburg, Billy and the band found fame and stardom in the UK and then America during the 'British invasion'. With fame and stardom comes women and partying, both of which I love. I know what I'm like. I don't think I would've been able to stop myself from overdoing it. Billy tasted success with The Dakotas, but it tested him greatly on a personal level. He survived those tests, but I'm not convinced I would've been so fortunate. Plus, if

I'd joined them, I wouldn't have my kids, and I would've missed out on so many other great experiences.

* * *

Brian Epstein is famous for being The Beatles' manager, but they weren't the only Merseyside band signed to his label. Far from it! And, as Brian's stable of talent grew, it increased the competition between the rest of the unsigned bands. Suddenly, to secure a booking at certain high-profile venues, bands were falling over each other to perform on an 'audition only' or 'expenses only' basis. This was often the only way we could be seen by a promoter without doing a cold audition. And, because the biggest bands in Liverpool would invariably be on the same billing, there was a guarantee of a big audience. You also stood a good chance of having your name published in The Liverpool Echo alongside the likes of Rory Storm or even The Beatles.

This new sense of competition had changed the atmosphere. We used to go out of our way to help each other. Now we were desperately battling to stand out from one other and land lucrative spots or management offers. Merseybeat had changed and I began to feel that the whole scene had gotten out of focus. Wasn't it only yesterday that NEMS music store had its first enquiry about Tony Sheridan records?

This loss of focus was summed up by a conversation I had with George Harrison. That night, we'd given Ringo a lift from Northwich Memorial Hall to the Blue Angel club, as we were all going there to hang out. 'From Me To You' had just hit the top five and 'Beatlemania' was really starting to take shape. Standing at the bar with George that night, I asked if he'd like a drink. He replied in a somewhat sombre tone: "If I buy all the musicians in here a drink, they'll call me a big-headed bastard. If I don't buy them a drink, they'll call me a tight bastard. How can we win? It's the same with the music. No one's listening. All the girls do is scream."

Despite all of his success, George Harrison never forgot me and my Cruisers. We were even namechecked in an interview he gave to Mojo Magazine after the Bangladesh concert. *"The morning after the Concert For Bangladesh was August 2nd, ten years to the day since The Beatles had played two shows at The Cavern; the latter in the company of Karl Terry and The Cruisers. And now, to borrow a John Lennon phrase, 'there was all this'. Having spent a decade running, it was probably time for George Harrison to slow down."*

That night at the Blue Angel, George, like the rest of The Beatles, was starting to see the writing on the wall. They were moving into a different stratosphere and it was going to take some adjusting to. We *all* had to adjust. Merseybeat bands may have been trailing in The Beatles' wake, but we were working hard to make the best of the sudden craze for all things Liverpool. It felt like this was our time! Everybody from Land's End to John o' Groats wanted a piece of the Mersey action (and accent). Promoters and agents were all looking for another Beatles and, as long as you came from Liverpool, the world was wide open to you.

It was a particularly good time to be a Scouser in London. I was invited there to have some of my original songs reviewed with a view to publication. You're always at risk of getting jerked around in London. Luckily, I had some friends, Dave Preston and Georgie Peckham, who lived there. These great guys looked out for me while I was in town. To my amusement, when we went to the *very* exclusive 'Speakeasy Club' near Oxford Street, I had absolutely no problem gaining entry. And, while trying to attract the attention of an aloof barmaid, Keith Moon of The Who overheard my pleading and offered to buy our drinks all night, simply because we were musicians from Beatle-pool. That night, Keith pissed in the water jug on the bar, mixed it into his drink, and complained about that drink to the aloof barmaid, insisting she taste it to see if it was alright... which she did.

As the fame of the 'fab four' spread around the world, so did the demand for any band that could duplicate their sound and mannerisms. In Manchester, The Hollies, Freddie and The Dreamers, and Herman's Hermits all got in on the act. Down south, the Rolling Stones, Brian Poole and The Tremolos, and Johnny Kidd and The Pirates were jumping on the bandwagon. Even American artistes like Gene Vincent, Jerry Lee Lewis, and Little Richard were becoming more Beatles-like.

I witnessed the shift in The Hollies' attitude first-hand, as their beautiful harmonic style altered dramatically within a couple of appearances at The Cavern Club. Their clothing changed as well. Suddenly they became very popular with audiences and Liverpool band members alike. I remember having a conversation with Allan Clarke of The Hollies, where he said that "front-line singers are finished". At that time, it was hard to argue. I became quite friendly with both Allan and his terrific drummer, Bobby Elliot, for a while. This was mainly over drinks in the Blue Angel. What a place that was!

The Blue Angel

The Blue Angel was a nightclub owned by one of Liverpool's favourite characters, former Beatles manager Allan Williams. Many writers have detailed Brian Epstein's management of The Beatles, but the influence, contacts, and opportunities Allan Williams provided are often brushed aside. Not by me. Allan was the one who travelled to London to meet with Manfred Weissleder, who was negotiating the supply of English groups to Hamburg. Howie Casey and The Seniors, and Rory Storm and The Hurricanes were already there blazing a trail and Allan saw the great potential of this scene. He took The Beatles there to get some experience and they came back a changed band.

Allan was so sure of success that he drove the band to Hamburg himself. He also took an experienced Trinidadian calypso player and promotor, Lord Woodbine, to act as a mentor to the young group. Remember, they were still teenagers at this point. The legend of Allan Williams doesn't stop there. Supposedly, he heard Pete Best practicing his drumming above a store in Bold Street and introduced him to the rest of the group. Sadly, when Pete was driven out of the band, Allan could do nothing to save him.

Allan went into club management, and his late-night spot in Liverpool's city center, Blue Angel, became the place to be and the place to be seen! This club was special because, as well as being a great music venue, it had an exclusive 'two o'clock bar' where bands wouldn't get bothered by fans and roughneck teddy boy types. Here, musicians, artists, poets, celebs, and a select few, all came together to appreciate each other and enjoy some great music. There were lots of women floating around, too, which was music to my ears.

If you were good enough and keen enough you could perform at Allan's club seven nights a week. The place was so popular that they had two bands playing at the same time on Friday, Saturday, and Sunday (one upstairs and one in the basement). And, after your gigs, you could hang out in the 'two o'clock bar', which was absolutely *the* place to be! Not only could we have a drink with fellow musicians without being bothered, as word got around that this place was special, impromptu jam sessions would take place there.

One memorable evening, my good friend Bobby Thompson arrived in the company of The Ronettes and The Bill Black Combo! He was also accompanied by various members of the Cliff Bennet Band, for whom he was playing at the time. This triggered an impromptu jam session that I'll never forget! That night, the house band allowed Rory Storm and Freddie Starr to voice a rendition of Ray Charles' 'What'd I Say', with Freddie outrageously imitating Rory's famous stammer! If I recall correctly, Mick Burt, Chas And Dave's drummer, was also there and played with us. Later that night, I was invited on stage to sing. I would be accompanied by Bill Black, Elvis's original bass player, and several other prolific musicians. My backing vocals came courtesy of The Ronettes! Wowser!

With the explosion of the Merseybeat sound, more and more celebrities visited 'The Blue', as we affectionately called it.

Among them were: Judy Garland, Bob Dylan, The Rolling Stones, and the cast from The Likely Lads. Local hit recording groups made a beeline to the club too. You wouldn't be surprised to see The Searchers, The Swinging Blue Jeans, The Merseybeats, Billy J. Kramer and The Dakotas, Gerry and The Pacemakers, and Cilla Black; alongside up-and-coming recording artistes like The Escorts and The Dennisons. And so, the legendary Blue Angel earned its spot in Merseybeat folklore. It certainly has a special place in my heart.

The Beatmakers

What The Beatles did today other bands copied tomorrow. And, as their popularity increased outside of Liverpool, so did their imitators. Of course, the original was always the best. That's why they sold out every venue they played at. From church halls to bingo rooms, cellars to civic centres, the atmosphere wherever they performed was special. Even without alcohol!

To be on the same billing as them now required a huge effort from the supporting bands. No matter how hard they tried, nobody could challenge The Beatles' unique harmonies or individual charisma. I, for one, decided not to imitate them and stuck to my own style. I think people respected me for that. That respect earned us the chance to appear on the same bill as The Beatles countless times. And it's probably the reason that I was asked to sing with them and The Pacemakers in the world's first 'super group'! Wowser! Wowser! Wowser!

Can you believe I'd almost forgotten about this event? I was only reminded of it years later at the reopening of The Cavern in 1984. Everybody who was anybody in the heyday of this famous venue was being interviewed at that time. By chance, Frankie Connor (of The Hideaways) and I were approached by Radio Merseyside for an interview. Our interviewer was the legendary former Liverpool footballer, Tommy 'The Anfield Iron' Smith (who went on to own and run the 'new' Cavern Club). During the interview, Tommy reminded me of my unique claim of being in the world's first super-group, The Beatmakers.

How could I forget such an occasion? Well, in our younger years, any band worth their salt could work maybe ten or fourteen gigs a week. You might start on Sunday with a gig at The Orrell Park Ballroom or Blair Hall and double that gig with an appearance at The Hollyoak Ballroom. Monday, you might play at The Top Hat Club on Lockerby Road or The David Lewis Ballroom or Wavertree Town Hall or The Majestic in Birkenhead. Tuesday might see you playing at The Peppermint Lounge. Wednesday, The Iron Door Club or Saint Luke's (a.k.a. The Jive Hive). Thursday, you could be back at Wavertree Town Hall, or the Odd Spot, or The Cavern, or the Iron Door, or maybe Columbia Hall in Widnes. Friday you're at The Cavern or The Prescot Cables Club and then on to New Brighton Tower Ballroom. Then, on Saturday you might be playing The Klick Klick, or maybe The Marine Club in Southport, then perhaps it'd be The Civic Hall in Ellesmere Port or The Ivamar Club in Ormskirk, and then you'd go on to an all-night session at The Cavern or The Iron Door or maybe both! That's on top of doing lunchtime sessions, birthdays, and weddings. When you've played that many gigs, things easily get lost in the mists of time.

However, it all came back to me the second Tommy brought it up. On that fateful night at Litherland Town Hall, October 19th, 1961, The Cruisers and I were bottom of the bill, and The Beatles and Gerry and The Pacemakers were top. However, rather than fulfil the usual billing, after our set had finished, the two major bands decided to collaborate for one night only. And, as my set was over, they invited me to join them as a lead vocalist. Wow! This hastily assembled band contained two drummers,

Freddy Marsden and Pete Best, two lead guitarists, Gerry Marsden and George Harrison, then it had Les McGuire on saxophone, Les Chadwick on piano, Paul McCartney on bass, and John Lennon on maracas and tambourine.

Boy, I wish I'd recorded this unbelievable and unique combination of world-renowned talent! It all seems like a dream now. How the whole thing sounded I'll never know, but it was received rapturously by the sell-out crowd. This wouldn't be the only time Merseybeat bands came together in this fashion. It happened many times in Hamburg at clubs like Der Kaiserkeller, Top Ten, and The Star Club. But we were the *first* super-group.

In retrospect, I realise that I actually played with The Beatles twice! The other occasion was at a club called The Mandolin and was organised from the Orrell Park Ballroom by the manager, Ken Hignett. This gig turned out to be an impromptu jam party, with band members playing different instruments and backing each other in mix-and-match line-ups. For example, I'd be on the drums while Pete Best sang, etc. That evening I played with every member of The Beatles at one point or another.

The drummer-go-round

As far as I'm concerned, the question of why Ringo Starr replaced Pete Best in the summer of 1962 can only be answered by three people: Paul, Ringo, and Pete himself. Heated debate still rages. For example, what was George Martin's role in the sudden change? And why, although involved, didn't Ringo drum on the original recording of 'Love Me Do' or 'P.S. I Love You'? Were the other Beatles threatened by Pete's popularity or was he really not up to the job in their eyes?

I played on the same bill as The Beatles many times, I hung out with them, and, as I just mentioned, I even played with them. Being in close quarters with them during this early period meant I was able to observe their chemistry first hand. I also got to see how crowds reacted to them, particularly the female fans. Anybody who was around in at the dawn of Beatlemania would agree that the vast majority of the female fans following the group were there for Pete!

Pete is a friend and remains the most approachable musician I know; always making time for a chat with fans or other musicians. But, all bias aside, the near riot that occurred when Ringo played at The Cavern for the first time as a Beatle tells you all you need to know. At that performance, in response to the fans repeatedly chanting "we want Pete", George Harrison replied: "Go 'round to 8 Hayman's Green (Pete's family home), you might get a cup of tea." Taking exception to this put-down, an ardent fan head-butted George Harrison and the band abandoned their second set. Pete was incredibly popular with the fans, which raises a question: If Brian Epstein was such a perceptive and astute businessman and manager, why did he get shut of The Beatles' biggest attraction? Did he think Pete would end up outshining the rest of the band? Or was he simply reacting to the other band members' concerns?

Whatever the reason, this development sent shockwaves through the industry. The overall consensus was that The Beatles had made a big mistake and had possibly lost seventy-five percent of their fan base. Once the shockwaves subsided, bands across Liverpool woke up to the fact that Pete was now up for grabs. Surely the band that recruited him would steal those alienated fans from The Beatles?! And so, the drummer-go-round began. I managed to find the funny side of this crazy period, but it did affect us. Having recruited Roy Dyke from a band called The Creoles, Roy and I were both asked to replace Faron and Don Alcyd in the T.T.s, which we declined. Then, Roy suddenly left us to join The Remo Four!

Rory Storm and The Hurricanes were caught right in the middle of the storm. This band were the undisputed flash-action group on Merseyside, and I strongly suspect that Rory's pioneering showmanship influenced Rod Stewart's glam rock and theatrics years later. Despite being a leading light, Rory was enduring the same frustration as me in the early sixties. The Beatles' grip on the direction of the music meant that the groups we'd constructed had quickly become old fashioned. Then, to add insult to injury, Ringo Starr left The Hurricanes for The Beatles!

The loss of Ringo hit Rory and his band hard, but the race

to fill the vacant seat was hotly contested. Even our Frantic Franz chanced his luck. It's worth mentioning that, despite the fact Rory could sing all night long and introduce all of his band's numbers, off-stage he had a terrible stammer. So, when our Frantic telephoned Rory to enquire about replacing Ringo, it cost him one whole shilling to hear a single word: "n-n-n-no". For a while, The Hurricanes seemed to have a different drummer every set. Some nights, while performing two or three gigs, Rory had several drummers queuing up to audition!

In the end, Jimmy Tushingham solved Rory's drumming problem and his band's energy and attack soon returned. Nobody could upstage the golden boy for gimmicks, either. I witnessed them first hand in my brief time playing with his band years later. This came about because they were missing a band member and I was in-between bands, so we helped each other out. I'll never forget a gig we played at Lytham Cricket Club. When I introduced Rory, the band immediately kicked in and he ran onto the stage. That stage had a low girder across the front which Rory swung from, landing on some guy dancing with his girlfriend. Rory received a kick in the face for his troubles. The golden boy also stole the show at an all-night session at The Cavern Club around Bonfire Night. That night, he ran onto The Cavern stage with some 'Bangers' (small indoor fireworks) and some 'Rip Raps' (a string of bangers) and completely upstaged all of the other bands sitting in the front row waiting to heckle him.

Rory's struggle to replace Ringo was typical of this uncertain time for the Merseybeat 'Top Twenty' group leaders. Friends on and off stage, we swapped tales of woe at the coffee bars, music shops, and swimming pools we all hung out at. One night I found myself on the same bill as The Big Three, which was a coincidence as I happened to be doing a bit of building work on the house of their drummer, Johnny 'Hutch' Hutchinson, while moonlighting as a brickie.

Chatting between sets, I was shocked when Johnny confided in me that The Beatles had asked *him* to join them before they asked Ringo. He declined their offer as he reckoned they weren't a patch on The Big Three. Rumour has it that Hutch wasn't the only one they asked, either. Then again, there were also rumours that, before joining The Beatles, Ringo had agreed to join Kingsize Taylor and The Dominoes in Hamburg. This was plausible due to Ringo's connection with their bass player, Bobby Thompson; a fine singer and someone who I greatly treasure as a friend. He and Ringo played with The Hurricanes on the American bases in France. This chaotic time would soon claim another victim as, in late 1963, The Big Three themselves split up. More shockwaves! With engagements still to fulfil, Hutch asked me to appear with him on the TV programme Scene At Six-Thirty because I bore a passing resemblance to Johnny Gustafson, his former band-mate.

Hutch was desperate to reform the band. He held auditions for potential new members while I was still working on his house. You wouldn't believe the array of well-respected talent who were prepared to quit their own outfits in search of success with the new Big Three. My close friend and mentor Lance Railton auditioned. As did the talented Wayne Calvert. Charlie Smullen, bass player with Cy Tucker and The Friars passed through, too. Eventually, the new members were announced. The fabulous Faron Ruffley, having returned from a stint in Hamburg with Gerry and The Pacemakers, was one. And my good friend Paddy Chambers was the other. Wowser, what a line-up! An all-new Big Three had begun.

Pete Best, after fielding numerous offers, joined Lee Curtis and The All-Stars. This was understandable as the group included talented songwriters like Tony Waddington on lead guitar and Wayne Bickerton on bass. Wayne would go onto great heights writing songs for Iguana, Katie Kissoon, and Tom Jones among others. And, filling the remaining gaps, The Fourmost ended up swapping drummers with The Dominoes. You might not be surprised to hear that, during these turbulent times, my band's existence was also in on a knife edge.

No longer cruisin'

Tragically, the original Cavern Club, Liverpool's most iconic music venue, was closed and demolished in the early 70s. They even ripped out bricks and pieces of wood from the original stage and sold them off as souvenirs. A decade later, somebody realised it would've been a good place for the ever-increasing Beatle tourists to visit. So, the powers-that-be decided to build a new Cavern Club! The week of the grand opening, illustrious Merseybeat names were invited to perform special gigs. These names included Billy J. Kramer, Gerry Marsden, George Melly, The Merseybeats, Faron's Flamingos, The Undertakers, and Karl Terry and The Cruisers! Wow!

During the opening of the 'new' Cavern Club in March 1984, the world's press once again descended on Liverpool. True to tradition, the band members were asked to sign The Cavern stage backdrop. A new 'wall-of-fame' was unveiled too; with the names of all of the groups who'd appeared at the original Cavern etched into the bricks. I count myself incredibly fortunate to have played in six bands on that wall: Karl Terry and The Cruisers, The Delameres, Amos Karl and The T.T.s, Karl Terry and The T.T.s, Rory Storm and The Hurricanes, and a band called Group One. Wowser! I could build my own wall with those bricks!

You might notice there are a lot of Ts in that list. The Ts

refer to the Tempest Tornadoes, which morphed from Johnny Tempest and The Tornadoes into Faron and The Tempest Tornadoes upon Johnny's untimely death from meningitis at the age of just twenty-one. I'd always had a close relationship with this band thanks to my friendship with their guitarist, Lance Railton. Lance's band were a great outfit, but they went through a lot of ups and downs; most notably when Faron Ruffley left to accompany Gerry and The Pacemakers to Hamburg. Faron was replaced by Earl Preston and Cy Tucker; after Roy Dyke and myself had declined the offer to lead the band at that time. Unfortunately, this charismatic line-up (that once challenged The Beatles' supremacy) lost their lead vocalists again! This time, Amos Bonny and yours truly stepped in. We morphed into Karl Terry and The T.T.s and then The T Squares, which contained half of the original Clayton Squares and half the original T.T.s. But before I joined the T.T.s I spent several months with a Geordie band called The Delamers! Still with me?

This band hopping came about when I put The Cruisers on hold during a tough period. We weren't the only band struggling to keep it all together, either. With the increasing scramble for a share of The Beatles' limelight, rash decisions were made; some good, some bad. The Merseybeats parted company with bass player and chief harmoniser (and really nice guy) Billy Kinsley. Billy, in turn, was replaced for a time with Johnny Gustafson from The Big Three, who then himself moved onto new ventures with Atomic Rooster, Roxy Music, Bullet, and even Johnny Kidd's backing band, The Pirates. Despite the stunning success of The Searchers early recordings, their lead singer, Tony Jackson, left the band, got a nose job, and formed a new combo, Tony Jackson and The Vibrations, which was far less successful.

The Swinging Blue Jeans also experienced changes. They

lost their drummer and lead guitarist, Norman Kuhlke and Ralph Ellis respectively, and replaced them with Kenny Goodlass, the drummer from The Kirkbys, and Terry Silvester *and* Mike Gregory of The Escorts. To accommodate these changes, Les Braid reverted back to playing the piano. But the changes weren't over, as Terry Silvester soon moved to The Hollies to fill the vacancy left by Graham Nash. Mike Gregory moved on too, heading to Big John's Rock 'n' Roll Circus. I think 'rock 'n' roll circus' sums up this crazy period quite well.

So, what happened to me and my band? Well, as the Merseybeat scene spread, the demands and decisions of promoters and band members became more and more farcical. One night, when we were up near the Lake District playing a gig in Barrow-in-Furness, having performed at the Carlisle Market Hall the night before, our band temporarily broke-up over an argument over a sixpence! This all began at Carlisle train station. You see, in the good old days before yobs and vandals took anything that wasn't nailed down, most railway platforms had a sort of vending machine where you could purchase cigarettes, chocolate, and milk. Would you believe me if I told you that the argument that developed between our bass player, Gerry Clayton, and our drummer Gordon 'Frantic Franz' Templeton, was all over the cost of milk?! Things quickly became heated.

During the argument, Gerry went to the toilet to piss and maybe take a moment to calm down. In those days, there were toilet cubicles on the railway platform that had an open roof and a large space at the bottom of the doors. Adjacent to this particular toilet were two fire buckets; one filled with water and the other with sand. In no mood to calm down, our Frantic decided to kick the door in and empty both buckets over Gerry. Perhaps you can you imagine those two lunatics chasing around the station platform; one of them dripping wet and covered in sand, with his trousers around his ankles.

It took the rest of the day to convince Gerry to continue the tour, but he did. When we finally arrived at the Duke of Edinburgh Hotel in Barrow-in-Furness, we found that there was no room for our band to unload our equipment and set up. It was the first time a Liverpool band had appeared there and they were unaware of what was required. Still, the crowd at the venue went crazy for us before we'd even played a note! Having never seen a reaction like it, the venue manager booked us for the following night on the spot.

Thinking on our feet, we got the audience to pass our equipment overhead to the stage and set up as best we could. It was a great gig, but it was chaos! And all this trouble for a fee of fourteen pounds. The venue manager had also overlooked the fact that Billy J. Kramer was appearing at the local ice rink the following night. We had no chance of competing with Billy's hit-record pulling-power and the crowd was considerably smaller.

From this point on, the atmosphere in the band had changed. We'd had plans to go back to France, but suddenly everyone was pulling in different directions and I was struggling to hold it all together. Then I received an offer from The Delamers that was going to be very hard to refuse. This was another crossroads in my career, but it felt like the right time to give The Cruisers rest and challenge myself in a new setting. It was a hard-nosed business decision too, as I'd be earning a much better living as a truly professional musician. My mind was made up. Karl Terry was leaving his Cruisers and joining The Delamers!

A Scouser in a Geordie band

I've talked about musicians finding musicians. Well, in nineteen-sixties Liverpool, they were most likely to be found in the Kardomah Café at the corner of Whitechapel and Stanley Street. It was near both Hessy's music store and Rushworth's music store, where The Beatles bought their Gibson Jumbo guitars. Its proximity to these fantastic music shops made it a big hangout for musicians. Members of almost every band hung out at the Kardomah Café and, for a while at least, we were like one big extended family. We even arranged a game of football every now and then! But, when The Beatles released 'Love Me Do' and appeared on Scene At Six-Thirty, everything changed. Bands sensed that fame might come calling for them if they could just stand out enough. So the competition became fierce and the friendly spirit became increasingly strained.

Regardless of the atmosphere, the Kardomah Café, or K.D. as it became known, was the place to be! Whenever anybody vaguely familiar walked in, some other group member would offer to buy them a tea or coffee and chat about their band. One fine afternoon, in walked a tall, sallow-faced stranger. Like most friendly Scousers, I started a conversation. Thing is, I couldn't understand a word he said. After enquiring if he was Greek, maybe off a ship docked in Liverpool, he slowed his speech and informed me he was a Geordie who the played bass guitar in a band. At this time, the only "bands" were dance bands. In Liverpool, we called ourselves "groups".

As the conversation continued, I learned that this guy's name was Dave 'Mac' McGibbon and that his band's leader was the lead guitarist and vocalist, Dave Shipperly. They also had Gordon Railton on piano and vocals, a drummer named "Icky", and a rhythm guitarist and vocalist named Colin Weems. They were working the Mecca dance hall circuit and had recently become the resident band at The Locarno ballroom. Mac asked if I'd like to come and hear the band? Man, was I in for a shock?! All of the Merseyside beat groups were. The Delameres could, and did, play any number of styles, including the nearest thing to the Everly Brothers I've ever heard. They had a powerhouse drummer and bass player, a terrific boogie-woogie pianist, and a brilliant lead guitarist. But nobody had heard of them until the fateful day when Mac walked into the Kardomah Café.

Before I move on, I have to share a funny incident involving the fabulously talented Freddy Starr. Now, the manager of the Kardomah could be quite strict and, for whatever reason, she had banned Freddy from the café. Not to be deterred, one lunchtime, he snuck in and hid beneath the counter. As soon as the manager went into the back room, Freddy sprang out of hiding and purchased a salad roll and a coffee. Of course, when she reappeared, she spotted Freddy immediately and told him to leave, which he did. But so did his cup and saucer and the plate with the salad roll on it. It was such a funny sight watching the manager chasing Freddy Starr across Whitechapel, trying to retrieve her crockery. God bless you, Freddy! What a unique talent and an outstanding personality.

Now, back to musicians finding musicians. Merseyside

bands were attracting a new, younger audience to all kinds of venues; from school halls and coffee bars to underground cellars and night clubs. Even the big dance hall companies like Mecca and Top Rank were phasing out the old big bands in favour of talented beat groups. One such beat group was The Delamares. And, as luck would have it, the friendship I'd struck up with their bass player, Dave 'Mac' McGibbon, lead to me being asked to audition for the band. Their rhythm guitarist had taken a day job with the Eldorado Ice Cream Company in Hughes Street, West Derby Road, almost facing the Locarno Ballroom. He was also busy courting a Liverpudlian girl, as many of the band were.

The Cruisers and I were in a bit of a lull, so, after a successful audition, I made a hard-nosed decision to join The Delameres. I'm glad I did, as playing with this talented band was an experience that I'll never forget. Another reason for joining this Geordie band was that my earnings suddenly rose from fifty pence an hour with my Cruisers to eleven pounds per hour with The Delameres. In fact, when we had a short residency at The Denniston Palais in Glasgow, our pay rose to thirty-six pounds an hour! My ambition of becoming a truly professional musician had become a reality.

That period in Glasgow was very memorable. The event promoters had put full-length posters on the street proclaiming that The Delameres were "direct from Liverpool"! With Beatlemania in full swing, hundreds of girls queued around the block expecting a Beatles-type group. When we eventually got into the venue, the manager went berserk when he discovered that four-fifths of the band were Geordies. He immediately stipulated that, as I was the only Scouser in the band, I was the only one allowed to announce the songs, otherwise we'd have a riot on our hands. True to form, as soon as I uttered *"aw'right der, luv?"* in my best Liverpool accent, the whole place went crazy. Thanks to The Beatles, the majority of the British public suddenly had a much higher regard for *anyone* with a Scouse accent; especially footballers, comedians, and musicians.

The job with The Delameres had its restrictions, though, as the band were contracted to Mecca Entertainments. This meant that any extra gigs were taken on solely at the discretion of the manager of the ballrooms. Naturally, with my contacts, I was able to secure gigs at places like The Cavern Club, The Iron Door Club and The Peppermint Lounge. Getting the Mecca manager to agree to us playing there was another matter! This wasn't the only problem, either. These famous venues that once opened their door to any decent band, were now establishing themselves as agencies and managers in their own right. This meant that they began to trade solely with each other; swapping their tried and tested bands between each other's venues.

Of course, these new agents and managers touted to secure gigs for their bands at The Locarno. Here, they witnessed for themselves the quality of the vocals and musicianship of The Delameres. As a result, Bob Wooler of The Cavern Agency, Les Ackerley of The Iron Door Agency, George and Jimmy Blott of The Peppermint Lounge Agency, Jimmy MacIver and Dougie Martin of IvaMar Entertainments, and, of course, Brian Epstein, all approached The Delameres to sign an exclusive contract. The problem was, with the guys being from Newcastle, they hesitated to commit to a contract in Liverpool that didn't have the guarantees of their contract with Mecca. They decided to stay on the Mecca circuit. I, on the other, hand wanted to be in Liverpool, as it was still 'happening' there. So, my time with The Delameres came to an end. But those wonderful Geordie guys, in addition to being superb singers and musicians, are some of the nicest people I've ever met and are true friends to boot.

When I returned to Liverpool, Faron Ruffley had just left the T.T.s to join The Pacemakers. This left my good mate Lance Railton, along with Dave Gore, and Wally Shepherd (Guitar, Bass, Rhythm) in the lurch. Ready to make a triumphant return to the Merseybeat scene, I agreed to front the T.T.s. My time with this great band, through its various guises, led to a combination of the T.T.s and the fabulous Clayton Squares down the line. But, in the back of my mind, I was always planning to revive The Cruisers. One day.

Memories of Madrid

In the mid to late sixties, the Clayton Squares were considered by many to be one of the best Merseyside bands. However, in 1966, after a successful period playing at the Star Club in Hamburg, things started to unravel among the band members and it was time for a change. I was drafted in to replace Denny Alexander as the band's lead singer. In doing so, I linked up once again with my good mate Lance Railton. Lance had been playing with the T.T.s until about 1963/4 and had switched to the Clayton Squares after a bit of band hopping. This new line up was full of stellar talent. In addition to Lance on guitar, Geoff Jones on bass, and Tommy Maguire on drums, we had two great sax players in Mike Evans and Albie Donnelly. In the years that followed, Mike would go on to be a respected music critic and Albie formed the celebrated band Supercharge. This group was talented, but it wasn't *the* Clayton Squares. So, in the spirit of the original band, we became 'Karl Terry and The Squares' and started playing gigs in Liverpool.

Our new group had secured a regular gig at the Blue Angel, which, as I've mentioned, was very popular with musical celebrities. Where the celebrities go, managers and agents often follow. Those agents were always on the lookout for new talent, and, if the house band was anything out of the ordinary, a deal might be struck for further engagements. One night at The Blue, Allan Williams introduced me to a guy who'd already taken several Scouse groups to Madrid in Spain. Having seen us play that night, he asked if we'd be interested in performing there on a two-week contract. At eleven hundred Pesetas a week, equivalent to seventeen pounds, the money on offer wasn't great. But with a little haggling, and the promise that we'd "live like kings", we agreed to leave for Spain the following night... *after* our performance at the Blue Angel!

* * *

Before the concept of a 'roadie' had been invented, every band had their one trusted friend. Ours was a great guy named Billy Joynson, who I met through Lance. Billy was in the Territorial Army and was just one of those really dependable people. Most guys in bands, certainly the ones I've been in, are pretty irresponsible, so it's great to have that kind of person around you. In fact, if it wasn't for Billy, our Spanish adventure might not have happened at all. Having never travelled abroad before, Billy was pretty excited. He took charge of the trip and decided he would drive us all the way to Madrid – even spending his own money on a mini-van!

Neither Billy nor I had any mechanical knowledge (I couldn't even drive!), but we purchased a Standard Atlas Van from Brunswick Street Motor Auctions. This motor looked trustworthy enough, and it was dead cheap, so who cared? Turns out we should have. As we neared London, the front wheel bearing collapsed. We had no idea what to do, but Billy took care of the repairs while the band retired to the pub. Now, getting musicians into a pub is easy, getting them out again is another matter! With the problem fixed, Billy managed to wrestle us back into the van and off we went again... for about a mile. Suddenly, the engine burst into flames! With no extinguisher to hand, Billy improvised and pissed the fire out, which we found hilarious. Despite these challenges, we arrived in Dover and were ready to set off on another European adventure.

Crossing the English Channel was just one of many new experiences for our 'Billy Big Nose'. This wasn't a happy experience, though, as he was struck down with seasickness just as we were about to drive off the ferry at Calais. I took over at the wheel, despite the fact that I had no license, insurance, or experience! The French Gendarmes surrounded our suspect vehicle almost immediately and escorted us to the customs shed.

We had a contract to appear in Spain and were only traveling through France, but the customs people would only allow the passengers and vehicle, no instruments. They were to be held in a bonded warehouse waiting for us to pay tax for their release. Otherwise, if we sold them in France, they would be worth three times their English value. With no money to release the instruments, we were still in Calais twelve days later! To make things worse, we were sleeping in our van and were covered in flea bites thanks to our saxophonist, Albie Donnelly, who'd brought a sleeping bag that his cat used to sleep on. Things got so bad that our drummer, Tommy, caught scabies!

This disorganised yet democratic band of musos-for-hire decided to pool what little money we had to form a daily ration that would keep us going until we could beg a cash advance from our agent in Spain. The problem with this plan was that, due to the Basque terrorist activities at the time, the French weren't accepting cash transactions from Spain. Typical! After some negotiation, it was agreed that we could arrange for a surety of fifteen-hundred pounds to be deposited in a Crédit Lyonnais Bank in Calais. This would be returned when we completed our, by now almost certainly defunct, contractual obligations and travelled back through Calais. A sound idea in theory, but we still needed to find fifteen-hundred pounds.

By this time, we'd boozed our way through our original traveling expenses budget, but our pooling system allowed us two-and-a-half French Francs a day per person. This meant I could buy a packet of cigarettes and a baguette so that, whenever I felt hungry, I could chew on some bread. This, I'd worked out, left me a little bit of money for a glass of red wine! Albie and Lance didn't smoke, so they just drank wine and ate baguettes or scrounged food as best they could. But during one drunken pub crawl, things got a little out of hand. For one, Albie, after a long 'conversation' with a deaf First World War veteran who wore a cloak like an extra from Beau Geste, somehow managed to purchase that cloak. Draped in his new finery, Albie stumbled on to the next bar where he found Geoff 'Bonehead' Jones, our bass player, stuffing his face with the finest French cuisine! It turns out we hadn't *all* been pooling our resources honestly. The remainder of our drunken Scouse clan returned to the clapped-out van and relieved cans of peaches and beans from Geoff's haversack.

After some frantic telephone calls, Lance's dad, good old George Railton, came to our rescue and wired us the fifteen-hundred pounds surety to release our instruments. And, once we were on the road again, we somehow managed to persuade two hitchhikers to fund our expenses to Madrid, as a loan, in exchange for a ride. And boy did we take them for a ride! There was space in the van because our *brassed-off* brass section, the welsh-clog-dancing Mike Evans and the now cape-draped Albie Donnelly, had decided to hitchhike to Madrid rather than risk it with us.

After a straight forty-eight-hour drive (during which we almost got turned back at the border because, after sixteen days without washing or shaving, none of us resembled our passport photos) we arrived in Madrid! I should mention that it was under the rule of General Franco at this time and outsiders weren't particularly welcome. This was made clear to me when I asked a guy with a bullfighter's hat and a rifle with fixed bayonet for directions to our agent's office. It probably didn't help that I was as hairy as a monkey's arse. Then again, in those days of long-haired lovers from Liverpool, I could hack it with the best of them. I wish you could've seen my (Elvis eat your heart out) sideburns!

Now the fun really began. As soon as we entered the agent's office, we learned, that the most important word in the Spanish language as far as he was concerned was: "Rapido!" He also informed us that our name meant nothing in Spain, so we'd have to change it to make it more relatable. Thinking on my feet, I came up with 'Karl Terry con Los Plazas', which translates as 'Karl Terry with The Squares'. Our Spanish agent accepted the new name and took us to our lodgings, or *la pensión*, which reminded me of a movie called The Colditz Story. Mike and Albie, who'd hitchhiked ahead of us, were already there. In fact, we turned a corner to find Albie prostrate on the bed with a bollock the size of a football! He'd been drunk the previous night and fallen down the hole in the toilet floor that he was supposed to be pissing in, almost rupturing himself in the process.

As we wouldn't get paid until we'd fulfilled our tenuous contract, we were taken to a bar where we could eat, drink, and smoke on a tab. That sounded good to us penniless musos. None of the people we dealt with in our hilarious three and a half months of Spanish chaos spoke English, and we quickly worked out that this communication issue worked in our favour. At the bar, we were required to sign credit chits for the meals, drinks, and cigarettes we were taking. No one ever asked for identification, though. So, musicians being musicians, we signed fake names. Even the non-smokers in the band were getting free cigarettes! This went on for a month; despite the fact that we'd been fired from the club after only two-and-a-half numbers!

How did that come about? Well, after traveling for eighteen days and nights, we were all pretty tired and hazy so we went for a drink. We didn't have much money, but this didn't stop us from heading to the first bar we could find. In this bar, Las Cuevas, the Spanish patrons were getting by on something they called *"vino grande"*, which seemed to be the cheapest, roughest red wine available. We soon realised that this demon brew, full of fruit that was instantly removed, would make our modest pile of Pesetas go quite far. As a result, our day sitting outside Las Cuevas bar in Spain's sunny capital was rather intoxicating.

When the time finally came to set up our equipment at the venue, a huge ballroom in Madrid, we were a little frazzled. We were even more frazzled when our drummer, Tommy Maguire, accidentally plugged our mains board into an Italian band's mains board! This blunder shorted something in the electrics and, somehow, caused to the stage curtains to open. This kicked off a big introduction for our band from Beatle-land and, before we knew what was happening, we were playing! Of course, all the audience could hear was two saxophones and a drummer thrashing on his kit, but 'the show must go on'! While we played, Billy Big Nose frantically tried to rectify the situation, and Lance Railton and I tried to cover up the fact our guitars weren't functioning by staging a fencing a duel with them. Unfortunately, in the melee, he managed to cut my chin with his machine head. Next thing we knew, the compare shouted *"muchos locos!"* and dropped the stage curtain on us. We were unemployed again.

Amid the chaos that followed, Albie informed us that he was packing up his saxophone and leaving. This was another big blow. But, just as things seemed like they were slipping away from us, a saving grace arrived. We were approached by a man who thought we were the best thing he'd ever seen. He offered us a recording contract to make an EP (an 'extended play' vinyl of around four tracks) for the 'Hispa Vox' record company. This guy was also was a double bass player at the top club in Madrid and was sure he could get us hired there. Boy, sometimes when your luck's in your luck's *in*. The next day we successfully auditioned at Club Imperator, and learned that the guy who owned that club also owned seven others. We instantly shot to the top of the bill and became his *"numero uno hombres"*. With free drinks to boot! Cuba Libres! And with each new round we toasted: *"muchos grathias señor!"* Of course, we all got *"muchos pissed"* too. Or perhaps that should be *"pithed"*?

Over the next few nights, word spread about this new sensation from Liverpool and we started to sell out the club... and the Cuba Libres. Business was booming and the queues got bigger and bigger. Everybody was happy, and why not? We were also still on credit from our first disastrous gig, because the agent was in Milan and didn't know we'd been fired. Wowser! The good times kept rolling, too. With our renown growing, we were invited to meet and greet the fabulous Tom Jones at Madrid airport! Photographs from this event were in all the Spanish papers, which in turn made us even more popular at Club Imperator.

It certainly wasn't all sunshine and *vino grande*, though. At one memorable performance, while I was busy trying to sound like Sam Cooke, Lance whispered "me stomach's aching" and calmly walked off stage while we were playing the last number of the set. When we came off stage a few minutes later, we found Lance on the dressing room floor with blood coming out of his mouth and ears. An ulcer had burst and he needed to be hospitalised immediately. It was during Lance's recuperation that we were invited to play at Tom Jones' club. When Lance heard about it, he pleaded with the doctors to allow him out for one night only. They did, which was a great relief to the band and myself in particular as I'd have my inspirational partner back on stage. It also freed me from having to play the guitar, which meant I could resume my lunatic antics.

Speaking of antics, the *"muchos locos Inglés"* weren't done yet. With Tom Jones due to perform at Club Imperator, a huge scaffold platform was erected on the existing stage so that all of the fans could get a clear view. We were the main support band that night and we were on fire! Inspired by my band, and me being me, there was no way I wasn't going to scale the heights on this night of nights. Up the scaffolding I went! Of course, I was duly reprimanded by the stage manager, but that performance caught the eye of Tom Jones' manager, who asked us to contact his office and arrange a management deal when we returned to England. We did end up signing with him, but this was three years later.

At the peak of our booming period in Spain we did a T.V. spot at the fantastic Teatro Zarzuela with the Rolling Stones and Sandie Shaw! But, soon afterwards, lady luck once again deserted us. Just two days before we were due to record our long-awaited EP for Hispa Vox, the Spanish Police marched into the club with fixed bayonets to inform us that diplomatic relations with Britain had broken down due to the closure of the border with Gibraltar. This relationship had lasted for thirteen years, why did it have to break down now? Just like that, our Spanish adventure was over. Now we had twenty-four hours to repatriate to Paris.

We were forced to take the train from Madrid to Paris, as Billy Big Nose, having spent most of our time in Spain refusing to drive due the dangerous roads and drivers, had driven another Liverpudlian group, The Handful, home instead of us! So much for our reliable friend! Thankfully, our journey to *gay Paris* was great fun. While we were exploring the train (looking for the bar, naturally) we bumped into some friends from a fabulous vocal group called The Chants. Together, we decided to buy a few bottles of wine to see us through the journey. Big mistake. We ended up getting so pissed that Lance pulled the emergency chain for a laugh. We must've been close to being *double* repatriated!

When we arrived in Paris, we had to lug our equipment down to the Metro. This was a sight to behold! Once we'd made it onto the Metro platform, we fashioned an arrangement whereby, as the Metro doors opened, two of us would stand inside the train while the other four would pass them our gear. But as soon as we'd thrown one drum case and a small bag in, the stupid doors closed and off went the train; leaving four pie-eyed musicians to haul the remaining mountain of gear. The plan was to return to Calais, tally the serial numbers on our equipment with the customs officials, and get George Railton's fifteen hundred quid back where it belonged. But, with a third of our group lost on the French underground, we weren't sure if that would ever happen.

Instead, we made our way to Le Havre, which is a long way down the coast from Calais. Once there, we hopped on to a ferry and found ourselves among lots of day-tripping French school children heading to Portsmouth. We also found our two lost band members on board. Now, we had our gear, our band, and a captive audience of school kids. Out came the guitars and soon the boat was rockin'! It was *rolling* too, as the English Channel was pretty choppy that day. One by one, the lads took on a whiter shade of pale; except for Geoff, who turned distinctly green and acquired a new nickname, 'The Mekon', after the Dan Dare comic book character with a big green head.

Arriving in Portsmouth was another barrel of laughs as we'd acquired a new band member! This guy, an escaped English foreign legionnaire, asked if he could join us for a drink. Well, at that time I was the only one able to converse with him as the other guys were in various stages of seasickness. The story went that this ex-legionnaire was escaping France and had smuggled himself on board. He asked if he could disembark as one of our band and we went along with it. Of course, he was rumbled pretty quickly on arrival, as he was the only skinhead among a band of down-at-heel hippies. A man from the Diplomatic Corps, along with reporters from the Sunday People, were there to greet him upon arrival. His story was all over the newspapers – not that *we* got any publicity!

Bad Vilbel (it's a town in Germany)

Within days of being back in Liverpool, our bass player, Geoff 'Bonesy' Jones, announced he was leaving. We quickly put the feelers out and replaced him with Gordon Loughlin. Then, after a couple of nights together at the Blue Angel, déjà vu struck. Allan Williams once again approached us with an offer of work abroad. He knew a guy with a club in Bad Vilbel, West Germany, who was on the lookout for Merseybeat talent. Allan was one of the most helpful and lovable guys anyone could wish to know; if he could help any band or musician he would. He brought this opportunity to our attention knowing that he would be losing one of the most popular acts at his club for a second time, but he did it anyway and we're forever grateful.

The German club owner was a guy called Bobby Blum. Allan had agreed a deal that required us to leave the following night; after we'd finished our gig at the Blue Angel at two in the morning! We would then travel by train to London (Billy Big Nose declined our offer), negotiate the underground, and proceed to the Dover to catch a ferry to Ostend in Belgium. Once there, we would catch the train down to Frankfurt in the American sector of southern Germany! Sounds easy enough. Lock up your daughters and your beer barrels, here we come!

Five drunken musicians set out for Liverpool Lime Street in

the dead of night. But, as we lounged there in a stupor, we realised that none of us had received our traveling advance from Allan or Bobby. We made a frantic phone call to good old Allan, who raced to the station, slightly inebriated himself, and handed over the money to cover all of our expenses, *plus eighty pounds extra*, which Lance calmly slotted in his pocket. Wapaloonie! Oh, and, for reasons that remain unclear, Allan also brought us a keyboard player, Chris Hatfield. We all knew Chris, but none of us had ever worked with him. As I say in these situations: "Rock 'n', roll, that's all." Our six-pack... sorry, *six-piece* band now consisted of: myself on vocals, Gordon Loughlin on the bass, Tommy Maguire on drums, the Welsh clog-dancing Mike Evans on saxophone, Lance Railton on guitar, and Chris Hatfield on Vox Continental organ.

Bad Vilbel is a beautiful little spa town. At least it was until *we* arrived. The club we were playing at was known as the Ritterkeller, and boy was this gig a blast. The club's owner, Bobby Blum, introduced us to his business partner, Karl Mildenberger, who was a European champion heavyweight boxer. In fact, Karl was the only white European to go the full twelve rounds with Muhammad Ali in his prime. No messing around with Karl then! Once we'd gone through the house rules and set-up our equipment we went to our hotel. This hotel was run by a sweet old lady, who was very efficient and *very* officious. She welcomed us as "mister Beatle boys".

I shared a double room with Gordon 'The Araldite Kid' Loughlin. He got that nickname because he had to glue his bass speaker cabinet back together every time he played. No sooner had we checked in, Gordon, who was by far the most considerate and conscientious person in the band, went to the local shops and returned with, what I can only describe as, a metal jug with a separate electric heater element. He plugged it in and made us both tea. Gordon had also purchased eggs, coffee, milk, cornflakes, jam, bread, and butter! Now we were cookin'! But what about the hotel rules? Turns out that sweet little old lady took no prisoners! When she discovered our contraption, a tirade of German profanity was fired at us and we immediately apologised and unplugged it. Unbeknown to us, Lance and our clog dancing saxophonist had purchased exactly the same bloody contraption! Not only that, they left it plugged in all night and then made the mistake of plugging their guitars in too, which almost blew the whole place up! Wowser! We were booked into this hotel for a five-week stay but got kicked out on day two; possibly setting a record for the shortest 'long stay' hotel reservation in history.

Lance was such an inspirational personality and musician; I think about my dear departed friend at least once every day. He was no Arnold Schwarzenegger, but he was also not a guy to be intimidated by anybody. So, when things started going south with our accommodation and our contract, Lance volunteered to confront 'The Great White Dope' of European boxing, Karl Mildenberger. We never found out the details of that discussion, but our new accommodation was a single spare room that was adjacent to the front door of the club's main entrance. It had two double beds (no mattresses) and a grill plate for cooking *and* heating.

Just when it looked like things couldn't get any worse, they did. It began to snow! At least we didn't have as far to stagger to our beds after performances; performances which Karl had now decided he wasn't going to pay us for! Instead, Karl decided he would give us free drinks all night. Naturally, we squeezed every penny out of this new 'arrangement'. For Lance, in particular, it was like giving strawberries to a donkey. He probably drank his own weight in cherry brandy! The rest of our outfit were no slouches either. I reckon the alcohol consumption of Bad Vilbel must've shot up tenfold while we were in town.

Being the most conscientious among us, Gordon 'The Araldite Kid' Loughlin, was entrusted with the *only* key to our front door. I say "front door", it was actually more of a stable door that was split horizontally into two sections, with the lock in the bottom half. You've probably guessed what was coming, but we didn't. The Araldite Kid lost the key! This meant that, if you passed by in the wee hours of the morning, you'd witness six drunken English musicians, wearing Sergeant Pepper-style jackets and high-heel platform boots, clambering over a stable door. What a scene!

* * *

When he realised his stage and dance floor were getting covered in glue from Gordon's bass cabinet (to the point that shoes were getting stuck) the club boss decided to buy our Araldite Kid a new Selmer 'Goliath' bass cabinet! "Rock 'n' roll, *das ist alles!*" Shortly afterwards, we were informed that a *real* professional group with *proper* equipment were coming to play at the Ritterkeller Club. Not only that, we were to do a ten-night tour with them! We were sent to Frankfurt's main rail terminus to meet and greet their road manager, 'H.', who was travelling ahead of the band with their 'professional equipment'.

With free beers thrown in, waiting around in Frankfurt rail station was no problem for six thirsty musos. When the train finally arrived, we watched the passengers closely as they alighted, but didn't see anyone with any instruments. Then the guard's carriage door opened and out flew five yellow Vox AC30 amps, with no speaker cloths, a microphone stand, and a full set of 'Trix

On Trixon' cone-shaped drums (with the drum skins removed so they'd fit inside one another). This was the equipment of a London-based band called The Pretty Things! Wowser!

The Pretty Things were booked to stay in the sweet old lady's hotel. We met up with them there on arrival for a press interview that included free drinks and refreshments (the perks of being a professional band!). At the hotel that night, the frontman of this band, Phil May, got so drunk that he stumbled into the wrong bedroom! There, he found a traveling salesman asleep and promptly dragged him out of bed. The salesman went running for the sweet old lady and, when she came up to investigate, Phil dragged *her* into bed with him! The Pretty Things broke our record for shortest stay.

Both bands sobered up just enough to set off on our ten-night tour – once we'd negotiated the stable door, of course! On the tour bus, the bass players sat with each other, as did the drummers, and I was next to fellow vocalist Phil May. The heavyweight champ loaded our gear onto the coach and announced: "We go. Everybody okay?" To which Phil replied: "Na, guv. We're ain't going nowhere 'til you put some booze on the bleedin' bus." With a mini-revolt on his hands, German Joe Palooka went back to the club and fetched some booze for The Pretty Things. But when they realised *we* didn't have anything to drink, they insisted he go back and get some for us too. A brave game to play, but it worked. With headliners and friends like these guys, we knew it was going to be a great tour! There's nothing better than being 'on the road' with guys you get on with. We had such a laugh. The tour whistled through Wiesbaden, Darmstadt, Höchst, Babenhausen, and Mainz among other places. But all good things must come to an end.

After their obligations were complete, The Pretty Things

went home and we returned to the Ritterkeller Club. We still weren't getting paid there, though. Unusually, this club had a stage that overlooked the whole length of the bar. There were no safety railings to prevent anybody from falling off onto the concrete dance floor below, either. This space gave me plenty of scope to loon around; swinging microphone stands above my head, sliding down the spiral staircase, or hanging over the bar like some drunken lunatic trapeze artist. The set-up also gave Lance the freedom he needed to, once again, take on our heavyweight host.

Guitar in hand, Lance somehow managed to climb down onto the bar (thank god he had a long guitar-lead or the whole bloody drum kit and P.A. would've gone with him). Now standing on the bar, Lance played one of the best solos I've ever heard him play. If you listen to his energetic break on Earl Preston and The TT's recording of 'Watch Your Step' you'll get the picture. He then proceeded to either drink or toe-punt the drinks that had been left on the bar. Wowser! Not satisfied, he then challenged European heavyweight champion, Karl Mildenberger, to a fight! This was on the condition that there would be no hitting on the face or hands as it would affect his performance. After all, he still had to play for the guy whose head he was threatening to knock off!

As you might imagine, our days in Bad Vilbel were numbered. They had to be! We had no chance of getting paid and the weather was getting colder. Plus, we were working six nights a week, with only Monday free. We also had to spend our days off at the club, as we didn't have the money to go elsewhere. Thankfully, our luck changed. A former saxophonist of The Clayton Squares, Les Smith, was living in Frankfurt while trying to solve the problem of perpetual motion (in addition to building an aeroplane) with his German friend, Dirk. Somehow, Les managed to get us an audition at the top club in Frankfurt, the

K52! So, one moonlit Monday night we hopped into Dirk's van and began leg one of our 'great escape'.

We successfully passed the audition at the K52 Club, but the guy in charge didn't have a slot for us for another two months! He could, however, offer us a guaranteed paying gig and a good apartment in Hanau, a town just east of Frankfurt. The clubs there were frequented by the American forces who had a base nearby. Suddenly, things were looking up. Our paying gig would start immediately. Then, in a couple of months, after a two-week break in England, we would spend a month performing in the top club in Frankfurt! First, we had to escape from our club in Bad Vilbel. We made another midnight dash in Dirk's van, only, this time we had all of our equipment with us. This included The Araldite Kid's new Selmer Goliath bass cabinet!

Soon, we were settling into our warm, clean apartment in Hanau. It had enough space that four of us could easily share one large room and the other two could share a smaller one. This caused a little friction, though, as Chris-the-keyboard-player didn't want to share with anybody but Tommy-the-drums, but Tommy-the-drums wanted to join the four pissheads in the other room. Despite these differences, Chris was a terrific keyboard player and did some of the best impersonations of Laurel & Hardy I've ever seen. After playing with us, Chris would go on to join Billy Fury's backing band and married the American R&B singer and songwriter Doris Troy!

Speaking of Americans, at that time segregation was rife in the U.S. and that segregation extended to the American forces. This was news to all of us, but not to our Welsh clog-dancing saxophonist, Mike, who always keen to take a commendable moral stand. In fact, when we once accidentally bought a pack of Peter Stuyvesant cigarettes (made in South Africa under the apartheid regime) Mike refused to smoke a single one, even though they were the only cigarettes we had. He also refused to play in the all-white American club, choosing instead to only play in the all-black one. Regardless of the club, most of the guys in the audience really enjoyed our band. Some of them even began to join us on stage; singing, drumming, or maybe bringing their own guitar to jam along. Though, as I write this, I wonder how many of those guys made it back to America. We all knew that, after Germany, their next stop was Vietnam.

* * *

Our two weeks in Hanau flew by. Thoroughly inspired, we returned to the UK for a short break to rest and prepare for our triumphant return to Frankfurt on April 1st. No joke! We made it back, but not without issue. It's never easy, is it? This issue had begun before we'd even left Germany for Liverpool. When we returned to England, Mike-the-sax decided to stay with Les and Dirk in Frankfurt. Since Mike was there, Les and Dirk offered to look after our band's equipment to save us from hauling it to Liverpool and back. Perhaps I should've seen the writing on the wall when two of our band members, Tommy-the-drums and Chris-the-keys, refused Les and Dirk's offer and took their kit back to Liverpool. Of course, just as we were approaching Liverpool Lime Street Station, both Tommy and Chris informed me that they would not be returning to Germany. *Nicht gut!*

We scrambled to find a new drummer and came up with Paul 'The Hitch' Hitchmough. After this job, I wouldn't see Paul again for twenty-three years! The renewal of our friendship was a complete fluke. All those years later, I bumped into Paul while waiting for a coach. I was taking my band to Bielefeld, Germany, where we were going to be a support act for The Undertakers and The Beryl Marsden Band. As luck would have it, The Beryl Marsden Band had employed Paul as their drummer. We were off to exactly the same place! I'm proud to say that Paul and I have been good friends ever since. He's still my first call when my band's in trouble and never fails to assist us if it's at all possible. But, when we first met, there was no time for rehearsals. Just pack your kit and go!

Liverpool FC legend Ian Callaghan MBE, alongside Jackie Kenyon, my sister Mo Price, and me.

In Hamburg, I finally got to meet Scotty Moore; Elvis Presley's original guitarist. I even had the chance to introduce him to my sons, Sean and Jonathan. A proud day.

Another treasure from Hamburg was meeting D.J. Fontana (middle left), Elvis Presley's original drummer! To the left of D.J. stands another great drummer, Brian Redman. And to the right, you'll see me and my good friend and promoter Horst Fascher.

A recent gig in Berlin. Yes, I can still do the splits!

It's not all flash action. I can do the slow numbers too.

Clowning around for the camera.

I finally met Bill Haley's Comets in person at The Cavern in 2004.
hese guys inspired me to become a musician, so meeting them
was a real honour.

I'll give any string instrument a go. Even a huge double bass!

This photo was on the cover of my 1994 LP, titled: 'Rock 'n' Roll – That's all'.

A special gig at The Cavern on New Year's Day in 2006, raising funds for New Orleans after Hurricane Katrina. Alongside me are Alan Gaskell, Joe Sunseri, and Alan Peters.

Not long after coming second in the Eurovision Song Contest in 1993, Sonia popped along to my gig at Hartleys Wine Bar in Liverpool. As luck would have it, I performed with Sonia long before she shot to stardom.

Pop star Craig Douglas and I at the Liverpool Olympia (Locarno ballroom in old money) on April 25th, 2008.

Sonia, long before she was famous, performing guest vocals with me and my band at Ogden's Social Club in Liverpool.

I had the pleasure of meeting Jim Bowen, legendary host of TV quiz show Bullseye, at the Floral Pavilion Theatre in New Brighton.

I shared a stage with Linda Gail Lewis, Jerry Lee Lewis's sister, at The Cavern Club in October 2004.

I performed on the same bill as Mike Pender of The Searchers
at the Royal Court Theatre in Liverpool.

A snap with the multi-talented
American teen idol Bobby Vee in
1996.

I met Chas, of Chas & Dave fame,
while singing at The Borderline
club in London.

I've always been a sucker
for a flashy suit.

A snap of my bandmate,
Ritchie Prescott, deep in the zone.
Ritchie played with The Pressmen
in the early sixties.

A gig at Hartleys Wine Bar in the Royal Albert Dock, Liverpool. The
band features Andy Bourne on sax, Ritchie Prescott on guitar, Kenny
Goodlass on drums, me on vocals, and Owen Clayton on bass.

Frankfurt

Our journey, for once, was relatively plain sailing… until the train's heating system broke down somewhere near snow-covered Aachen. By the time we arrived in Frankfurt we were frozen to the bones, but we eagerly turned up for our first afternoon session at the K52 Club. The club boss read us the house rules, which were fine, but our performing schedule was a head-scratcher. We were contracted to play *seven* three-quarter-hour spots between three o'clock in the afternoon and five o'clock the next morning! We also had to work out what to what the hell we were going to play for so long, and how to play it! 'The show must go on', and it did. Hour after hour. But, during our fourth set, something happened to the depth of our sound. Playing for such long periods was causing Paul's ankle to strain and he was struggling with the bass drum peddle. Not that he got much sympathy. During a break between songs, I heard Lance inform The Hitch: "if you can't play the peddle, kick the f***ing drum or *I'll* f***ing kick *you*!"

The band endured a few long, character-building nights, but things were starting to come together where the music was concerned. However, due to the long hours we were playing, our equipment was overheating and starting to break down. The band members weren't faring any better. I developed a sore throat pretty quickly. This probably wasn't helped by constant drinking and smoking. I'd smoke as many different brands of cigarette as I could lay my hands on. This included a German brand called Roth-Händle, which was comparable to those potent French cigarettes, Gauloises. You can imagine the kind of damage I was doing to my voice in the fourteen hours we'd spend in the club each day, never mind the long-term effects.

After maybe four nights I had to take a break from the vocals. That's when the fun began! No matter who you are in the music game, chances are you'll need to be creative with the truth at some point – it's just like being a politician! It wasn't just my vocal ability that had deteriorated, Mike's lips were split so badly he was unable to play anything but solos, and Lance was unable to use his left hand as his fingers were cut due to his energetic playing style. So, we decided to show our *versatility*. This took the form of Mike singing a couple of things, like 'I Got My Mojo Workin'' or 'Mellow Yellow'. Then, with some encouragement, I convinced Lance to sing Johnny Burnette's 'Honey Hush', along with a nice reworking of Carl Perkins' 'Matchbox' and Buddy Holly's 'Think It Over', while I played lead guitar. We scraped by.

One of the great things about playing at the K52 was that other bands appearing around Frankfurt were always dropping in to hang out after their gigs – the club was open until six o'clock in the morning after all! While we were there it became a hang-out for the likes of Gerry and The Pacemakers, The Hollies, and another Liverpudlian group, The Thoughts. These guys would drop in for a drink, or a chat, or maybe just to wind down after performing some long nights themselves. During one of these meet-ups we learned that, up north, in the wild swinging town of Hamburg, you could go to the chemist shop and purchase pep pills that would give you the energy to play all night long! The next day a couple of our guys gave them a try. Were they alert?

Sure! Alert to the need to run to the toilet every five minutes! Nobody had bothered to inform them that, for some reason, laxatives had recently been added to the pep pills. Wapaloonie!

I recall another hilarious moment in our drug-taking 'education' that occurred in Germany. Our lesson came courtesy of our new roadie, Dirk, the perpetual motion seeker. Perhaps it was for stress, or just for inspiration, but Dirk was into marijuana. One sunny day, heading to one of our engagements with The Pretty Things, we got stuck on the driveway of our venue (a big, gothic town hall). Hundreds of Pretty Things fans were swarming around Dirk's Volkswagen minibus, making it impossible for us to progress further. So, with the sun beating down on us, and the sunroof open, Dirk produced a beautiful silver pipe. He then loaded it with marijuana, expertly lit up, and handed it to Gordon, our Araldite Kid. But instead of inhaling it, Gordon exhaled and blew Dirk's precious marijuana up and out of the sunroof! Not so rock 'n' roll.

Our engagement at the K52 Club was fun from start to finish – even when the club boss accused us of playing *jazz* not beat! One night, I stood next to that same club boss at the urinal. He gave me a strange look, as though he knew me from somewhere. It was probably because our band was still on stage performing while I was in the pisser. Oops! In another memorable episode, we had a party of well-to-do people sitting ringside one evening. Their table was littered with wine and champagne bottles and the accompanying glassware. As the night wore on, this group became increasingly boisterous. Eventually, a lady from their group, who was as drunk as a skunk, made a bee-line for the stage to join in with Lance's solo. Although the stage was almost at floor level, she approached it head on and, instead of using the stairs, stood right in front of it. Lance, guitar around his neck, carried on like a true professional until, in her enthusiasm, this pissed lady somehow grabbed hold of Lance and pulled him, along with his guitar, amplifier, and microphone stand, off of the stage and on top of her. They fell together onto the ringside table, smashing the bottles and glasses to smithereens. It just goes to show you never can tell!

Another fact of the entertainment game is that you never know who might walk in off the street. At the K52 Club, all manner of visiting bands would drop in after filming a television spot or promoting a record. One special night, in walked a lady who, for my money, has made some of the most outstanding records ever to hit the charts. This was the fabulous Aretha Franklin! I like to think that she enjoyed herself almost as much as we did that night. You see, whenever a visiting celebrity appeared to enjoy our act, it was always an added bonus if we could encourage them to guest for one or two numbers. And, on this occasion, the goddess of power vocals came up and sang with us and blew the roof off! Of course, I then had to follow her incredible guest performance. How do you follow Aretha Franklin?!

Since that wonderful night, the only lady I've heard who could match Lady Aretha was Barbra Streisand. I witnessed the power of her vocal gift up-close when I appeared as an extra in her movie, Yentl. The final scene of this iconic film was shot, would you believe, on an Isle of Man ferry on the River Mersey! How did I end up appearing in Yentl? It's all thanks to the wonderful actor and musician, Ricky Tomlinson. Back in the day, Ricky was a plasterer and a musician and I was a bricklayer and a musician, so we knew each other well in both walks of life. When Ricky opened a casting agency several years later, he put us on his books as a band that could play in the background of things. But he also got me jobs as an extra. That's how I ended up bobbing about on a boat in the Irish Sea with Barbra Streisand. What a talent! And what a voice! Wow!

We were having a great time at the K52 Club, but things weren't always easy. For example, no matter how many times we hauled our kit to the repair shop, the amps kept breaking down. If it wasn't for the assistance of a great bunch of guys from Sheffield, we wouldn't have lasted as long as we did. These guys were sharing the billing with us in a band called The Prophets. They were the salt of the earth and had no hesitation in lending us their equipment. Their bass player, Moe, was particularly kind and always did his best to help, especially when we got fired. That's right, fired! After twenty-one days and nights at the K52, the club boss gave us the bullet, because, to repeat his words: "You play jazz, not beat." *Raus!* At least we got paid. We also got another job thanks to our good friends The Prophets.

They introduced us to a guy called Jim Curnutt, an ex G.I. who I called 'The Colonel'. I'm no Elvis, but this guy was no Colonel Parker either. That said, the man did at least try. He installed us in a nice hotel in Mainz called Der Mainzer Hof (which we re-christened '*their minds are off*') and cut a deal at the local army base. Here we'd have to sing for our supper, quite literally in my case. The main drawback, among others, was that this supper was *always* chili burgers. How can you live on those?! The tension was building among our band members too following several incidents involving 'Lancelot The Knave' (a new nickname for Lance).

I've never known anyone who could stay up all night and still get up at the crack of dawn like Lance would. And it didn't matter what state he'd been in the night before, either. When we travelled to the beautiful town of Bingen for a gig, the quiet consensus was that nobody wanted to share a hotel room with Lance. He could be a lot of fun, but he could also be a giant pain in the arse if you wanted to sleep and he didn't. Before checking in, we had to do a sound check at the venue, The Casino Royale. Despite his deficiencies, Lance was smart, perceptive, and a very talented guy – I can vouch for him showing George Harrison a few intros and licks in our younger days. On the way to the sound check, we looked out of the windows at this picturesque town on the steep banks of the River Rhine. When we got a chance to walk around town, Lance observed: "It's a bit like Chester, with all these gargoyles and buildings over-hanging each other." The hairs rose on my neck. He was so perceptive. "You know", he continued, "this is Transylvania territory; Dracula country". I replied: "He won't get me. I've got my silver cross and chain on". I wear that same cross to this day.

Room-sharing deals were quietly cut while we returned to our hotel, which was an old stable with a pretty cobblestone courtyard. While I was busy registering everybody at the reception desk, the other guys paired off and left me with Lance. It ended up being one of our more memorable stays. From our window, Lance caught sight of a large, gothic church on the side of a nearby hill. This place looked, in his words, "like Hassle Castle". He begged me to go and visit it with him the following night. The vampires and bats wouldn't come out in daylight after all! Lance had a great sense of humour, so I laughed it off and it didn't get another mention that night. However, bright and early the next morning, about six o'clock, he woke me up to ask me if I was Catholic, which he already knew, and then asked if it was Palm Sunday or something? "You arsehole", I replied. "Are you completely off your head?" But Lance was so insistent, as only *he* could be, that I had to get up and find out what the hell he was going on about. When I got out of bed, I froze. Every window and doorway in town had a garlic cross above it! Lance was right, this *was* Dracula country! The locals weren't taking any chances, either. Wowser!

The gig in Bingen was a great success. And, as the main bar in The Casino Royale was called 'The Bar of a Thousand-and-One Drinks', The Hitch did his best to sample each and every one of them! Unfortunately, he made the mistake of drinking with Lance. This would usually be fine, as we all got along well together, but Lance had developed a nasty toothache which The Hitch insisted could be cured by swilling ice-water. It couldn't. The shock caused by the ice-water got on Lance's nerves in every possible way. He flew into a temper and almost ripped the ice-cold tooth out of his head. He then turned his attention on The Hitch. Fortunately for Paul, and anybody else who was within flying fist range, we managed to restore order with the offer of another round of drinks.

Lance and I went back a long way, and I was often the only one who could calm him down. Sometimes, however, even I just got out the way! God bless him, though. He was my mucker and I treasure the short time we had together. We eventually solved his toothache when we got back to Liverpool. Lance was moaning so much that his father asked me to accompany him to the dentist. This dentist, the only one available at short notice, was known as 'the mad rush-in' (Russian). Scouse humour! I'm apprehensive about dentists, even when they're not treating *me*. Lance wasn't faring any better. However, the guy in the white coat assured us that he couldn't do any extractions without a further appointment. So, like a lamb to the slaughter, off went the Lance for his 'examination'. Seconds later, he ran past the waiting room, shouting: "Pay the bastard, he just took it out without saying anything!"

* * *

The Colonel, Jim Curnutt, got the message that we weren't prepared to exist on chili burgers for the rest of our lives. To counteract our murmurings of dissent, he arranged to take us all into Darmstadt to purchase new equipment. This included a brand-new Ludwig drumkit for The Hitch and new P.A. system for the band. We didn't have to sign any agreements or pay any cash, not that we had any. But I should've listened to those little warning bells ringing in my head, as we still had to live on bleedin' chili burgers.

Another great escape was in the offing, only this one didn't go quite so smoothly. The Colonel had arranged a gig at our hotel in Mainz. Sensing an opportunity, we put a plan in motion whereby Dirk, the perpetual motion seeker, would be ready with his van when the gig finished. Funds were tight, so, to pay for the fuel to get the minibus to Ostend and back, I offered Dirk my treasured boots to sell. Our plan was sound, but, as usual, all hell broke loose.

A couple of days before the great escape, Lance woke me predictably early with a request. Because I was "handy with my fingers", he wanted me to have a go at fixing his beloved cowboy boots! I won't print my reply. Those boots, to give you some context, had been worn constantly since he'd purchased them in Spain more than six months previously! But, my main man needed help, and I knew he'd do the same for me, so I gave it a go. The only tools I had to work with were a spoon and knife from the hotel dining room, but I got to work digging through the thick layers of sweat and grime on the inner sole of his boot. That job would've been hard enough for a cobbler, and I'm sure even Uri Geller couldn't have worked with this spoon after I'd finished with it, but God loves a trier. I found what was causing the problem and removed what can only be described as a greasy, multi-coloured lump of paper.

The boot was cured! But what had I removed? While Lance paraded around the room like General Custer, I unwrapped the grotesque matted object. Little by little, I began to uncover writing that read: 'Einhundert'. As this beautiful blue paper unfolded, Lance's eyes opened wider and wider. I'd uncovered *two* one-hundred Deutsche Mark notes! No chili burgers tonight! Suddenly, Lance remembered what he'd done...

At the 'A-Bar' in Hanau, one of the German bar staff took a liking to our cowboy-booted hot-head and invited him back to her mother's for a roast dinner. As he was half-pissed, Lance agreed. But when dinner time rolled around he changed his mind and did a runner! When last sighted that day, Lance was hanging out of the back of a taxi shouting: "Teggsy, where's me blower?" Teggsy was his nickname for me (derived from Terry). His "blower" was his inhaler, as he suffered from asthma, or "wheeze bang" as he called it. That night, the silly tosser put his money in his boot for safekeeping. Of course, being full of ale he forgot all about his stash of cash and it became part of his boot. Wowser!

The next day, while the guys and I were walking around the town, we witnessed the surreal sight of the barmaid from our club *rip* what was left of Lance's denim jeans from ankle to waist. She then pulled him inside a store. They re-appeared minutes later dressed in the coolest maroon-and-grey-striped, flare bottomed hipsters. Taken aback, we all jeered and blew raspberries, but this new look set a standard for the rest of us. In fact, as soon as Lance disappeared around the corner, we all rushed into the same shop to have a look. The Araldite Kid even bought the same trousers! Boy, did we all look sweet that night at our gig at The Star Palast in Raunheim! Twelve years later, I received the only known photograph of these clothes from Albie Donnelly. Albie found the picture stuck on a dressing room wall when he was playing at the very same venue with his great band, Supercharge. Ta, Alb!

Lance, the man with the money, bought all kinds of goodies for the six of us. This included a block of the vilest smelling cheese known to man, which we left outside of our Welsh clog-dancing counterpart's window. There, it baked in the sun until it was the rarest *rarebit* he'd ever smelt! Our new found funds also meant we could definitely get another 'great escape' underway. The plan was supposed to go like this: After the gig, which was upstairs at Der Mainzer Hof hotel, good old Dirk would park his minibus outside a window near to the stage. Then, while seemingly packing our gear away, we would discreetly lower the kit into the van through the sunroof and skedaddle to Ostend to catch a ferry home! A fine plan, in theory...

Things took an unexpected turn that night. Anyone who's ever seen me on a stage knows that anything can happen. In the middle of this particular gig, caught up in a solo, I began to twirl the microphone stand around my head as if I was about to throw the big hammer at the Highland Games! Of course, the base of the mike stand comes flying off. Everything seemed to be in slow motion as this heavy thing bounced dangerously down the middle of the great long tables. I swear to God, if it had hit anybody it would have killed them instantly! Thankfully, it didn't, and the crowd went wild; cheering and screaming for the band. Then they started smashing the chairs up and were encouraging us to do the same. It didn't take much to get us going. The whole band got in on the act! But, before we realised what was happening, the chef came running out of the kitchen with a *huge* cleaver in his hand. Wowser! Exit stage left.

How the hell we got out of there alive I'll never know. What I do know is that somewhere in southern Germany there's a Fender Tremolux amp-top with a little chrome plate screwed to the top, inscribed: 'Lance T.Ts'. That's in addition to my Selmer Selectortone amp. If anybody out there finds it, I've still got the H.P. agreement papers! At least The Hitch managed to keep his Ludwig kit!

When we reached Ostend the following day, we paid Dirk for his troubles and gave him my f***ing suede-riding boots as a bonus too! Then we set sail for Dover knowing that our German adventure was over. But I always sensed I'd be back.

Back to reality

Back at the Blue Angel, preening like Peacocks in our dodgy shirts and even dodgier flared hipsters, we had to face reality. The music scene was evolving quickly and the new style didn't suit us. The soul scene, which I didn't have the voice for, was booming and we were also up against the underground sounds of bands like The Electric Flag. Cool new trends like Ska, Motown, Blue Beat, 'free love' and hippies were suddenly all the rage, and here I was playing fifties-style stuff.

I re-launched The Cruisers, as I had always planned, but with the Merseybeat scene out of fashion and fast on the decline, finding our audience became increasingly difficult. With a family and a house to pay for, I did what I could to keep The Cruisers going, but I found myself having to work the band in around bricklaying jobs and vice versa. We also found that the only way we could convince new audiences to listen to our *original* songs was to announce them as the latest track from modern artistes like Wilson Pickett or Mose Allison.

Opportunities were slipping away from us, but it wasn't all doom and gloom. A small tour was arranged for us to support the Liverpool Poets: Roger McGough, Adrian Henri, and Brian Patten at the UFO Club in Tottenham Court Road, London. But this was a very different scene to what we were used to. The club had strobe slides and lighting that was definitely *not* rock 'n' roll. This was the shape of things to come. During this period, bands were getting louder, guitar solos were becoming ten or maybe twenty minutes long, and no one was interested in hearing Elvis sing 'That's All Right Mama' or Carl Perkins singing 'Matchbox'. Even Gene Vincent was now appearing in cabaret!

Times were getting tough for old rockers like me, but the show went on. We played on the Cumbrian coast at the Tow Bar Inn, then to travelled to Scotland to play at venues like Castle Douglas Town Hall. While in Scotland, we travelled right up to the north west for a gig in a port town called Kishorn. The port was famous for launching oil rigs and for being the filming location of a film called Zeppelin, starring Michael York. We then headed to Wales to play at Winkups Caravan Holiday Park in Abergele. We played eighteen consecutive Tuesday nights there; in between the Bingo and other assorted holiday camp acts. Of course, this was a far cry from our heydays in The Cavern, but we were keeping the music alive.

* * *

During 1989/90, with a new Cruisers line-up, I once again returned to Germany. The Merseybeat scene was, and still is, alive and kicking there. This time we were in Bielefeld to support The Undertakers and The Beryl Marsden Band, who featured my old friend, Paul 'The Hitch' Hitchmough, on keyboard. Being a supporting act has never fazed me because I love the challenge of getting a crowd going. We were taking a bit of a risk with this gig, though, as we'd be working with borrowed equipment and living off virtually no money as we wouldn't get paid until we'd completed our first gig. But at that gig we were on fire and the reception was amazing! We made such a good impression that we became the headline act the following night!

This was at a huge university, with maybe three thousand people dancing and enjoying a night of Merseybeat and rock 'n' roll. The guy who organised the gig, Manfred Kuhlman, would later become my manager and very close friend. He gave us such a triumphant announcement before our entrance that night, that hundreds of people to swarmed to the stage to see the 'Sheik of Shake' perform! But that performance, no matter how triumphant, wasn't without incident.

It began innocently enough. The night before, Manfred had taken some of us and our wives out for a meal. Conscious of the fact that our evening had run rather late, Manfred arranged for a taxi to take us to the gig at the University the next day. However, all hell broke loose when we arrived. My guitarist, Paul (aka: The Drunk Punk), had consumed almost all of the free beer that had been left in the dressing room for *all five* bands. A heated debate, to put it mildly, ensued. The lead guitarist from The Undertakers, a real gentleman by the name of Geoff Nugent, offered his services as a replacement, but the Drunk Punk somehow convinced me that he could play the gig. We declined Geoff's kind offer and took to the stage.

So, Manfred brought the house to a standstill with his big introduction and the excitement in the venue was incredible. However, as we struck the first chord, Paul drunkenly lurched across the stage and knocked our bass player, Waldo, and his amplifier flying! The crew and I did our best to divert attention and keep the show going while we repaired the amp. Then, from nowhere, we heard the tortured sound of Paul's Fender Telecaster, miles out of tune, kick into Dave Edmunds' version of 'I Hear You Knocking'. Our drummer and alto saxophone and did their best to keep up with him, but we were stumped.

I'll never know how, but I managed to pull the whole thing back together. Dressed in a pink suit with a black shirt and luminous socks, I performed my full arsenal of stage antics; karate kicks, the splits, you name it! We won the audience over and won Manfred Kuhlman's admiration in the process. Manfred and I built up such a good rapport that he became my manager and a very, very good friend. He's secured countless gigs for me and my band since and I'm forever grateful.

* * *

A few years later, in 1994, we were in Bielefeld once again to support the release of my first album, *Rock 'n' Roll – That's All*. As part of the promotion, we were booked to play at a prestigious gig full of well-known musicians at the Jazz Club in Bielefeld. As word spread that our album was recorded in Germany and that we were the last Merseybeat band still recording on vinyl, local and national newspapers, along with radio and television stations, arrived to cover the event. Following lots of interviews and photo sessions, our manager, Manfred Kuhlman, was approached by one of the television companies to record us playing live the following morning in The Jazz Club. The program would go out live as a sort of 'what's on in entertainment' around Germany. We agreed and, despite being rather worse for wear from the night before, staggered and fumbled our way into The Jazz Club the following morning.

We were greeted by the club management, along with camera and lighting crews, sound engineers, directors, their assistants, a catering crew. It was the whole nine yards! After a sound check and a dress rehearsal, the television station's reporter, who must've seen us the night before, asked me to do the most dynamic performance possible! Realising that my looning around was probably the reason we'd secured the TV slot in the first place, I agreed. But there was a problem. Most musicians will agree that it's very hard to be 'loose' for a performance in the morning; particularly when there's no audience to work with. Having explained our predicament to the reporter, I asked if the band could have a couple of beers each. Fine, but the club's bar was locked-up tight. Manfred, wanting us to give our best performance, took the initiative to dash out to the local shops. He returned a few minutes later with two crates of beer in typically large bottles and the band and I wasted no time in tucking into them. Ten minutes later I was on live TV doing my handstands and splits and twirling microphone like there was no tomorrow. It was a great performance and everybody was happy. While the crew packed up, we changed into our street clothes and had a little beer to celebrate. Then the house lights came up, revealing that the beer we'd been drinking to loosen up was alcohol-free! Makes you wonder.

In retrospect

When people ask me "how good were The Beatles?", I ask them to try and count the number of artists who've covered their songs. It's an impossible task because the list is endless. And it's worth remembering that, in addition to thousands of bands, instrumentalists, and solo artists, the list includes superstars like Ray Charles, Frank Sinatra, and Elvis Presley! The Beatles have even inspired songs themselves, like Dora Bryan's 'All I want for Christmas is a Beatle' and Little Jimmy Osmond's 'Long Haired Lover from Liverpool'.

You don't become cultural icons by accident. They had the style, the mood, the sound, the charisma, the humour, the glamour, and, most importantly, the talent. But in 1960/61 they were just another beat group from Liverpool. Besides Brian Epstein, who would've imagined they would go on to have such an influence on the music industry? Their trendsetting even transcended music; spreading into the realms of fashion and politics. They had kaftans, moustaches, and beards long before the hippies, and pretty much launched the flower power movement with 'All You Need Is Love'. Brian Epstein's prophecy more than exceeded itself. He thought The Beatles would eclipse The Shadows and Elvis. In the end, they were "more popular than Jesus".

Without the 'fab four' making Merseybeat an international sensation, who knows what path my life and career would've taken. All I know is, it's one thing to find yourself in the right place at the right time, but you've still got to have the talent to make the most of it. That's why I don't criticise or hold anything against any of the bands that got national or international attention. I learned that trait from my old gran, who was very down to earth. I remember sitting with her while we watched Frankie Vaughan on the television. Frankie was old hat to me. "He's crap him", I said. My gran replied: "Yea, but you're sitting here watching him. He's on the television and you're not." She was right. You can't knock somebody who's successful. Even the one hit wonders still had a career off the back of it and you'd swap places with them in an instant.

Instead of pondering all of the 'what ifs' of my career, I like to think that, thanks to being part of the Merseybeat scene, I've had experiences that most people couldn't dream of. In fact, writing this book has brought back memories of the hundreds of celebrities I've met over the years. When I'm asked to name the most famous person I've met, people expect me to mention The Beatles. But I think of this question in terms of *my* musical idols. For that reason, Gene Vincent is at the top of my list. He's the most versatile singer I've ever heard and I'm still mesmerised by him. But, as the saying goes, never meet your heroes. I was hugely disappointed when I met Gene in early 1962 at the Liverpool Locarno. He seemed drunk and had put on a lot of weight. Seeing him in this state was a real let down, particularly as I greeted him holding my entire collection of his singles, EPs, and LPs. Even so, he's my number one, and always will be. And, in case you were wondering, he did sign my records.

Another name on my list that surprises people is Elvis

Presley's original bass player, Bill Black. I met Bill the night Bobby Thompson invited Cliff Bennett's Rebel Rousers, The Ronettes, and The Bill Black Combo for a late-night drink at the Blue Angel. I was equally elated to meet Elvis's original guitarist, Scotty Moore, too. Scotty was such an inspiration to me and many other guitarists. What a player! Even my youngest son, Sean, copies his style and licks. One of the biggest thrills of my life was not only to meet Scotty, but to introduce him to my two sons, Jonathan and Sean. This was after a show at The Neptune Theatre in Liverpool.

Meeting Elvis Presley's first drummer, D.J. Fontana, was another dream come true. And a nicer man you'll never meet! I bumped into D.J. at an outdoor gig in Hamburg when the Cruisers and I were the opening act for The Everly Brothers, Brenda Lee, and All the Kings Men (featuring Scotty Moore and D. J. Fontana). Standing next to D.J. after a sound check (and a little liquid courage), I asked how things were going. "You guys sort'a blew us all away there for a while with all that 'ooh stuff'". He was refereeing to The Beatles and the way they used to shake their shaggy hair.

I told D.J. that my band were *still* trying to do what he, Elvis, Scotty, and Bill had been doing fifty years earlier. He seemed completely flabbergasted! I said, if he had the time, he could watch my performance to prove how genuine my words were. That night I very nervously sang 'That's All Right Mama', 'Baby Lets Play House', and 'Baby I Don't Care'; three rockabilly Elvis tracks that Scotty and D.J. were hugely influential in. When I came off-stage, D.J. immediately came over and said: "Hey man, you're a really nice guy." I'll take this to my grave! Back at our hotel, I posed for a photograph with D.J. and Horst Fascher. Horst, a good friend and wonderful promoter, looked after us all with equal courtesy and respect. Thanks Horst. God bless you.

Those guys are all at the top of my list, but I've had brushes with many famous faces who would be at the top of most people's lists. I met Bob Dylan outside the Blue Angel. We spoke, but I didn't manage to get an autograph. I saw Buddy Holly and The Crickets outside Beaver Radio Spares on Whitechapel in Liverpool. It still annoys me that I was so star-struck I couldn't bring myself to speak to them! But I did get to meet The Crickets nearly fifty-years later at The Cavern Club. Tom Jones was a joy to meet and work with when we were in Spain. I met The Rolling Stones in the Blue Angel, and several times after that too. And, fulfilling a lifelong fantasy, I eventually met the great Lonnie Donegan at Derby Lane Conservative Club. The man had so much time for me, it was amazing! He even autographed my ten-inch LP, then enquired if I had a spare copy to sell him. This was a real honour for me.

Perhaps, most importantly, after nearly fifty years of trying to sound like them and imitate their arrangements, I finally met Bill Haley's Comets! These were the guys who'd turned me on to the 'western swing' style with their recording of 'Green Tree Boogie'. I first saw them perform at the Liverpool Odeon picture house on London Road. I've still got my entrance ticket in a picture frame alongside The Comets' autographs and photographs. Wowser, what a band! I'll never forget that night at the Odeon. It was the late fifties, but it seems like yesterday!

The house lights were up and most of the audience were queuing up to buy an ice cream or a Kia Ora drink. I noticed a group of guys on stage with their backs to the audience. Then, over the sound system came those distinctive words: "*On your marks (On your marks). Get set (Get set). Now, ready? (Ready! Go!). Everybody razzle dazzle...*" The house lights dimmed and there they were: tartan jackets, double bass, saxophone, the full works! Rudy Pompilli, Franny Beecher and Bill Haley put on a stunning demonstration of how to present an act. During that performance, the bass player straddled his bass and split his trousers! The whole place went berserk, including me and my mate John Dickson. That swinging rhythm had us jiving in the aisle. We were only thirteen, but I decided then and there that, one day, my band would play like The Comets.

So that's where it all began for me, and I'm still living that dream to this day. That's why it feels strange writing a retrospective. My story is still going! And, while the heyday of Merseybeat is in the past, the music is enjoying something of a revival and finding a new, younger audience. Naturally, the majority of the people who come to see me and The Cruisers are roughly the same age as the band. Who could blame anyone for wanting to have a dance and relive a cherished part of their youth? But, every now and then, we play an event for younger crowds who are discovering our music and seeing it with new eyes. They tend to be part of the emerging rockabilly scene and seem fascinated and inspired by rock 'n' roll of all kinds. They even dress in clothes inspired by the fifties and sixties! I've played at these kinds of events in places like Leeds, Doncaster, Sheffield, Milton Keynes, and Great Yarmouth. Alongside the live music, they're selling records and memorabilia and the whole scene feels alive again. It's wonderful to see and be a part of.

As you can probably tell, The Cruisers and I are still playing gigs all over the United Kingdom and Europe. I'm among the last survivors of an era when Liverpool was the centre of the rock 'n' roll universe, and I'm honoured to be invited to almost every Merseybeat event going. They can't get The Beatles, The Pacemakers, or Cilla Black anymore, but they *can* get someone who was there; someone who lived and worked alongside the biggest names and more than held his own.

Perhaps I never achieved the fame and fortune they enjoyed, but I'm still here getting paid to do what I love. It doesn't matter whether you're playing for a hundred thousand people or a hundred, you still get the same buzz. Plus, when I travel to Hamburg and other cities on the continent, I'm treated like a king; with flights, food, travel, and accommodation all paid for. And then they pay you for playing! You can't beat that.